IDIOT'S GUIDES.
AS EASY AS IT GETS!

D0506253

JN27

Organizing Your Life

by Cyndy Aldred

A
ALPHA

A member of Penguin Group (USA) Inc.

ALPHA BOOKS

Published by Penguin Group (USA) Inc.

Penguin Group (USA) Inc., 375 Hudson Street, New York, New York 10014, USA · Penguin Group (Canada), 90 Eglinton Avenue East, Suite 700, Toronto, Ontario M4P 2Y3, Canada (a division of Pearson Penguin Canada Inc.) · Penguin Books Ltd., 80 Strand, London WC2R 0RL, England · Penguin Ireland, 25 St. Stephen's Green, Dublin 2, Ireland (a division of Penguin Books Ltd.) · Penguin Group (Australia), 250 Camberwell Road, Camberwell, Victoria 3124, Australia (a division of Pearson Australia Group Pty. Ltd.) · Penguin Books India Pvt. Ltd., 11 Community Centre, Panchsheel Park, New Delhi—110 017, India · Penguin Group (NZ), 67 Apollo Drive, Rosedale, North Shore, Auckland 1311, New Zealand (a division of Pearson New Zealand Ltd.) · Penguin Books (South Africa) (Pty.) Ltd., 24 Sturdee Avenue, Rosebank, Johannes- burg 2196, South Africa · Penguin Books Ltd., Registered Offices: 80 Strand, London WC2R 0RL, England

International Standard Book Number: 978-1-61564-648-7
Library of Congress Catalog Card Number: 2014941123

16   15   14   8   7   6   5   4   3   2   1

Interpretation of the printing code: The rightmost number of the first series of numbers is the year of the book's printing; the rightmost number of the second series of numbers is the number of the book's printing. For example, a printing code of 14-1 shows that the first printing occurred in 2014.

Note: This publication contains the opinions and ideas of its author. It is intended to provide helpful and informative material on the subject matter covered. It is sold with the understanding that the author and publisher are not engaged in rendering professional services in the book. If the reader requires personal assistance or advice, a competent professional should be consulted. The author and publisher specifi- cally disclaim any responsibility for any liability, loss, or risk, personal or otherwise, which is incurred as a consequence, directly or indirectly, of the use and application of any of the contents of this book.

Most Alpha books are available at special quantity discounts for bulk purchases for sales promotions, premiums, fund-raising, or educational use. Special books, or book excerpts, can also be created to fit specific needs. For details, write: Special Markets, Alpha Books, 375 Hudson Street, New York, NY 10014.

Trademarks: All terms mentioned in this book that are known to be or are suspected of being trademarks or service marks have been appropriately capitalized. Alpha Books and Penguin Group (USA) Inc. cannot attest to the accuracy of this information. Use of a term in this book should not be regarded as affecting the validity of any trademark or service mark.

Publisher: Mike Sanders

Executive Managing Editor: Billy Fields

Development Editorial Supervisor: Christy Wagner

Senior Designer: Rebecca Batchelor

Production Editor: Jill Thomas

Layout: Ayanna Lacey

CONTENTS

KITCHEN 29

DINING ROOM 53

LIVING AND FAMILY ROOMS 67

BATHROOMS 87

LAUNDRY ROOM. 111

CLOSETS 125

BEDROOMS 151

NURSERY......... 179

PLAYROOM 189

OFFICE........... 201

MULTIPURPOSE ROOM......... 227

GARAGE.......... 247

THE REST OF YOUR LIFE.................261

INTRODUCTION

Over the years, I've found that traditional ways of organizing don't work for everyone. With busy families, lots of hobbies and extracurricular activities, and often very little storage space, it's no wonder we struggle to try to create a sense of order and organization in our homes and lives. I've read almost every organizing book and magazine and incorporated so many of the ideas within them into my home. I've bought all the expensive organizational pieces. Yet for so long, an organizing solution that *really* worked for me and my family eluded me.

I got so frustrated I couldn't get my home and family organized, I finally had a realization. It occurred to me that I was working against myself by buying storage pieces that were forcing me to put things away in a very neat and tidy way. I can admit: as a family, we're not neat and tidy people all the time. We find ourselves tossing items quickly as we put them away, so bins and baskets out in the open—not storage pieces in which everything has to be neatly tucked away in its specific place—are better for us.

It's never been in my nature to put things away in an overly neat way. Add my busy family, with very little free time to put things away in an overly orderly fashion, and it's easy to see how organization methods that don't really work for us fail when we get busy.

Traditional, mainstream organizing systems tend to be designed for people who are good about putting things away neatly in tidy organizational pieces. Think about it: isn't that what the "after" photos often look like in organizing magazines and on storage solution websites? These might be the ideal for some, but they're not necessarily the solution for everyone.

I've found that there are myriad effective ways you can organize "out in the open," without having to neatly tuck things away using pretty pieces and creative strategies to finally get organized. As you look through this book, you'll see a common theme: most of the concepts are designed for realistic, out-in-the-open organizing opportunities that still look beautiful and provide a sense of order.

Instead of focusing on trying to force yourself into becoming a neater person who can use all the neat and tidy organizing ideas that look nice and mimic the popular magazines and websites, allow yourself to organize your home and life by focusing on how you naturally put things away. This has worked for my family. I hope it works for yours, too.

I hope I've inspired you to think differently when it comes to your stuff, your storage, and your organization and to discover the solution that finally works best for you.

ACKNOWLEDGMENTS

Thank you to my wonderful team at Alpha Books for all your work helping make this book the best it can be: my editors, Billy Fields and Christy Wagner, and designer, Rebecca Batchelor. Thank you to my amazing husband, Pat, and our beautiful daughter, Bella, for your love, patience, encouragement, and understanding throughout this book writing process. I know it wasn't easy, and I cannot thank the two of you enough for being so understanding. I am so grateful and thankful each day for your love. Thank you to my family for all your love and support—and yes, Mom, thank you for taking dictation for me on long drives. To my second family, the Shepherds, thank you from the bottom of my heart for all your support, dinners, laughter, and help with my crazy projects. Thank you so much to my dear friend, Amanda Carol Eck, for helping me talk through so many details when it came to this project. Your friendship has meant the world to me in so many ways. Thank you to my friends for your tremendous support and encouragement, and a very special thank you to my best friend, Sharon Hunter, for always cheering me on, talking me down from ledges, and being the best listener I have ever known. A very big thank you to all my favorite bloggers and designers who so graciously agreed to share a project (or two) in this book. Each of you has given me so much creative inspiration over the years, and I could not imagine doing this project without including the people who inspire me! Thank you so much ladies! Thank you to my contractor, Jesús Terrazas, for helping me through countless projects and brainstorming with me through all my ideas. Thank you to my readers of The Creativity Exchange. You have brought me so much joy and encouragement over the years. I thank each and every one of you for your support. I hope more than anything that through this book, you will see that organizing your life is very doable and doesn't have to be complicated. I hope that through this book and the projects shared, you, too, can find long-term solutions for getting and staying organized.

Once I realized I was going about organizing my home and life in a counterproductive way, I found inspiration, ideas, and creative solutions that fit the way I needed to think about organizing online from real life people with the same struggles I was having. These bloggers and designers, featured throughout this book, have given me tremendous inspiration over the years because they consistently and continuously share realistic, out-in-the-open organizing ideas that focus on maximizing space in functional—and pretty—ways. I encourage you to visit all the websites of all the contributors shown throughout for more ideas and inspiration.

GETTING STARTED

Are you ready to organize your life? If you picked up this book, that's a sign you're at least thinking about it, if you're not completely ready to jump in just yet. But even if you are ready to jump, sometimes the thought of getting your house and your life in order still feels so overwhelming. Where do you begin? How do you get started? How do you go about tackling all the areas of your life and home that need to be organized? That intimidating and overwhelming feeling you might be experiencing right now is the primary reason why so many people give up on getting organized before they even get started. But you don't have to be among them.

You *can* get organized. You *can* have a home that's orderly and organized. You *can* get your life on track. You just need some help, and that's what this book provides. In these first pages, you learn how to change the way you think about organizing; look at why you might not have succeeded at past attempts at organization; and begin to think differently about your stuff, your home, and your life.

RETHINK ORGANIZING

We all have unique ideas of what "being organized" means—your definition is probably different from mine, and neither of our notions is exactly like our friends', our neighbors', etc. And that's okay! We all approach organization and order differently.

Maybe you've tried to get organized in the past but soon fell back into your unorganized ways. Maybe you finally got your bedroom closet in order but ran out of energy after tackling that time-consuming project and didn't make it to the rest of your home. Or maybe you walked into your spare room, garage, or basement; saw the piles and stacks of stuff; and gave up before you even began to make some sense of the mess. Whatever you might have done in the past, that's in the past. Now you have an opportunity to make a clean start.

First things first, know that you don't have to live up to those perhaps-unrealistic visions of organizing perfection from pretty magazines that show everything in its place, or those equally gorgeous organizing websites that can serve as inspiration … but also intimidation. It's wonderful that those images inspire you, that they make you want to make some changes in your home and your life, that they make you want to finally tackle your lack of organization. That's what they're supposed to do.

But your home and your life are *your* home and *your* life. Neither must exactly match what those organizing experts have done—and probably have done with a large budget and styling professionals to help make everything magazine photo–worthy. Your version of being organized should be what works best for you, your family, your home, and your life.

The most important thing right now is to throw out any and all preconceived ideas and unrealistic expectations you might hold of what getting organized means to someone else, and with a clear, objective, unbiased view, pinpoint the trouble spots and areas in your home and life that slow you down. Once you can honestly identify these areas, you are better equipped to find and create long-term solutions you can stick with.

What those solutions are for you, you have to determine. (But don't worry, this book can help!) The key is to think differently, to approach the idea of getting organized without those past thoughts and memories of failure to weigh you down and make you discouraged. You can do this. You can get your home in order, whether that's a one-room studio apartment or a six-bedroom home in the suburbs. Almost all the ideas and tips in this book can be applied to whatever size home you have if you get creative and use what works best for you.

You *can* get your life under control. You *can* get organized!

photo credit: beneathmyheart.net; courtesy of Traci Hutcherson ▶

You don't need any special tools or knowledge to get organized. Sure, some baskets, bins, racks, etc. can help you tidy up your stuff and find homes for formerly homeless items, but you probably have much of what you need already that can be repurposed into new roles. By reusing what you have, you can corral your clutter without bringing yet more stuff into your space.

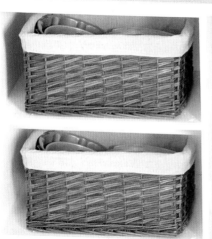

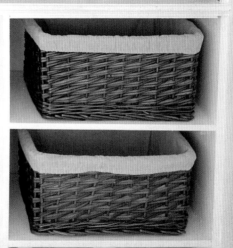

NARROW YOUR FOCUS

The busier your life gets, chances are, the more you long for some sense of order and organization. We all get to that point from time to time. It's a natural part of being human and dealing with all the "stuff" that accumulates around us.

In fact, you've probably sat down at some point when you felt the most unorganized and compiled a long list of all the areas in your home and life that need to be organized. (My editor is nodding her head as she reads this, thinking of how many extensive to-do lists she has at any one time.)

This "long list" approach, of writing down the often-overwhelming number of areas that need to be fixed, is the biggest reason why so many of us fail at organizing before we even get started. Few things are more intimidating and daunting than staring at that huge list and thinking about what needs to be done.

So don't do that. Instead of trying to organize multiple areas at one time, narrow your focus. Instead of thinking of all the problem areas in your life, work on resolving one issue at a time. If you focus on your number-one problem, you can channel more of your time and energy into not only organizing that area but also ultimately creating a long-term solution you can maintain.

WHAT'S YOUR NUMBER-ONE PROBLEM?

As you begin to think about organizing one problem area at a time, determine where the greatest source of frustration and disarray is in your home or life. In what area of your home, for example, do you waste the most time, or what rooms or spots do you seem to be organizing over and over? It might help to ask yourself, **If I could just organize one area in my home, what would that area be?** Chances are, you'll be able to answer that question instantly. If you can't, ask for assistance in identifying problem areas. Query your spouse and other family members on what they feel are the greatest organizational problem spots in your home. Including the family in your quest for order and organization is critical because you can't implement real, lasting solutions without their help. If you're still feeling overwhelmed and having difficulty pinpointing your primary problem, you can compile a short list—emphasis on **short**—of five of your greatest trouble spots. Then, prioritize your short list of five to better assess your main problem area.

The added benefit of focusing on one problem at a time is that there's often a chain-reaction effect. If you create a solution for one problem, you most likely will resolve other problems and address trouble spots, too, even if inadvertently. For instance, say all your craft supplies are stored in your laundry room cabinets. If you create a dedicated storage area for your crafting supplies somewhere else in your home—in your office bookshelves or your guest bedroom closet, for example—you simultaneously create new storage space in your laundry room. When you move your detergents, cleaners, and other laundry supplies into their rightful place in the laundry room cabinets, you free up space elsewhere in your home for other items to move into.

And notice those words *create a solution*. If you're constantly organizing a trouble spot, you're only providing a temporary fix. Instead, you need to create a solution that resolves the need for repeated organizing. Often, such cases are caused by a lack of something. For instance, does the area need an extra shelf or a unique storage piece to house stray items? Look for ways to go beyond simply organizing by determining what's needed and creating a long-term resolution.

By narrowing your focus to resolving one problem at a time and eliminating the overwhelming long list, you also allow yourself a victory one project at a time. All those small victories add up and give you the confidence and encouragement you need to tackle the next challenge.

photo credit: iHeart Organizing ▶

THINK CREATIVELY

The right solution for a trouble spot might not necessarily be a traditional item used for organizing. Remember, you don't need any specific or special tools or equipment to get your home and life organized—although you're certainly welcome to purchase bookshelves or matching bins or baskets to house your unruly stuff if that's what works best for you. However, if you solely rely on such traditional organizational pieces and hope they solve your problem areas, you limit your chances of finding the perfect solution for your unique issues.

Your organizational challenges are unique to your home, and one-size-fits-all organizational pieces are not guaranteed to resolve your trouble spots. Rather, the perfect solution could be that old dresser taking up space in your garage or a stack of garden pots your spouse was about to toss in the garage.

If you can look at your storage pieces, furniture, and accessories with an unbiased view of what they have been and instead focus on what they could be, if you can learn to think of them as prospective solutions to your organizing challenges, you can begin to think differently about organizing. That's how you find your creative solutions. If you train yourself to look first at the pieces you have already, you have the potential of doubling your efforts by fixing an unorganized trouble spot *and* creating additional storage space by using a piece that was taking up space elsewhere.

Oftentimes, the solution to an organization challenge seems a lot more complicated than what it really is. Many solutions are possible simply by tapping into your creativity and through do-it-yourself (DIY) projects. If you create your own solutions, you can customize them to maximize your specific space and address your home's unique areas. Plus, by reusing something you already have, you eliminate the need to buy more stuff and save money.

If you can change how you think about organizing, you can eliminate any preconceived notions you might have and learn to create real, long-term solutions. Instead of organizing something over and over, you can focus on finding unique solutions to resolve your home's and your life's unique, underlying problems. The result will be not only getting organized, but *staying* organized.

For too long we have been taught to hide and neatly tuck away clutter. However, for a busy family, the chances of keeping everything tidy behind closed doors is next to impossible. Instead, if you creatively incorporate storage solutions into your décor and out in the open, in every room of your home, you stand a better chance of getting—and most importantly, **staying**—organized. By placing creative storage solutions front and center, you and everyone in your family can see and understand where things go, where to return items when they're done using them, and where to go to look for something the next time.

HOW TO USE THIS BOOK

This book was designed to be a workbook you can use to get each area of your home and life organized and in order. Throughout are myriad tips, tricks, tools, and shortcuts to walk you through the organizing process, step by step, room by room, project by project.

At the beginning of each new section is an introduction to that room or area of the home, with notes on the key elements and points to ponder when it comes to organizing that space.

Then the fun begins. Using hundreds of photos, we show you fresh and fun ways to get organized. Throughout, I've tried to highlight some of the more creative options I've found to inspire you to think of unique solutions that might work for you, your home, and your organizational style. Although some of what's shown throughout these pages might not work for you, I hope they encourage you to look at your situation differently to see what other opportunities you can come up with that work in your space.

We've also included printable labels, worksheets, lists, and other items throughout the book to help you get—and stay—organized. These are available—for free—at thecreativityexchange.com/organizing-your-life.

At the end of each section, a handy checklist recaps important tips, offers links you can visit online for more organizing inspiration, and provides an area where you can jot down notes and things you want to try.

I'm a big fan of do-it-yourself (DIY) projects, especially those that help me control clutter, maximize the space I have to work with, and find a unique solution to a storage or organizational problem. I've shared several of my favorite DIY projects throughout the book. Some of these you can implement in your home as is; some you might need to adapt to fit your specific space. At the very least, I hope they show you that you don't have to be a professional organizer or an experienced contractor to create long-term solutions to the organizational challenges you face.

You don't need a lot of tools or specialized equipment to get organized, but I've found that some items are especially handy:

- A **tape measure** that fits on your key chain is one of my favorite things. When I'm out shopping for storage and organizational pieces, this is almost always with me and I can quickly check to ensure something will work in and fit my space.

- **Sticky notes,** stuck on the pages of this book or others, can help you keep track of your favorite ideas.

- A **camera,** on your phone or a standalone digital camera, comes in handy for taking shots of the room or space you're organizing so you can refer to it while you're out shopping for storage pieces. Or you can snap quick photos of potential storage pieces while you're out shopping to see how they'd look in your space.

I like bookmarks. They mark my page when I'm reading novels, they flag something I want to come back to later, and they encourage me to focus on only one problem at a time. To that end, I've created a bookmark for use with this book. If you slide it in the section of the book that corresponds to your number-one organizational issue, it can help remind you not to get off track or overwhelmed by the other areas in your home that need organizing. And the tips on the bookmark are the key elements to think about and ask yourself as you begin to think about organizing a room. To use the printable, go to thecreativityexchange.com/organizing-your-life, download the file, and print it on $8^1/_2$x11-inch (21.5x28cm) paper.

ENTRYWAY AND EXITS

Entryways especially but also exits are prime dumping ground for clutter as people come into, and go out of, your home. These areas are also easy spots in which to corral the clutter— the coats, backpacks, bags, hats, shoes, keys, and all the other little things found here— before it enters your home. If you can create good storage solutions right inside the door, you can prevent these items from cluttering other areas of your home.

In this section, you learn that even in the smallest and narrowest of spaces, you can implement easy and creative storage opportunities in the entryway and exits. The key is utilizing walls and other commonly wasted areas.

◀ photo credit: Amanda Carol Interiors

1 **LARGE BASKETS**
Large baskets are a great piece for any entryway. They provide decorative and practical storage and serve as a handy catch-all for tossing shoes, scarves, and books into.

2 **SMALLER BASKETS**
A smaller basket, box, or tray on a table is the perfect item for storing mail, keys, and other little pieces.

3 **WIRE BASKETS**
Wire baskets are useful for housing magazines, books, or other objects that need to be easy to see.

4 **URN OR LARGE LANTERN**
Urns or lanterns by an entry or exit can be used to store umbrellas without the worry of wet floors.

SMALL ENTRY

1 WALLPAPER

Wallpaper or paint can help define a small entry from the main living area, helping what's housed in the entry feel more organized and in the correct place.

2 SMALL CONSOLE TABLE

A small console table, or a narrow dresser, can create additional storage in this compact area. Also, having a tabletop right inside the door serves as an easy catch-all for mail, keys, etc.

Create even more storage by utilizing the space on top of and under a table in your entryway by adding trays, baskets, or bins.

◀ photo credit: Sherry Hart

THE
COAT WALL

1 **WIRE BASKETS**
Wire baskets can be utilized over and over again. They enable you to see what's in them at a glance so you know exactly what's where.

2 **HAT HOOKS**
Small hooks, installed in out-of-the-way spots, hold hats, earmuffs, etc. up and out of the way.

Corral scarves, mittens, shoes, travel bags, and other potential clutter in baskets.

3 **DOUBLE HOOKS**
Don't limit yourself to single hooks. Double hooks let you hang like items together without the possibility of misplacing anything.

4 **SHELVING**
Shelving provides additional vertical storage for baskets, buckets, or bins.

Easy Coat Wall

If you have a narrow entryway, you might not think you have room to get this area organized. But you can! This 3 foot, 6 inch (1m)-wide hallway is right by the back door—the perfect spot to hang jackets, backpacks, hats, and baskets for little things like scarves, mittens, travel bags, headphones, etc.

MATERIALS

1×6-INCH (2.5×15CM) PINE BOARDS

8×4-FOOT (2.5×1.25M) BEAD BOARD PANELING

1×2-INCH (2.5×5CM) BOARDS

FINISHING NAILS

CAULK

PAINT

COAT/HAT HOOKS

SMALL HOOKS

SCREWS

BASKETS, BUCKETS, AND OTHER STORAGE PIECES

TOOLS

PENCIL

TAPE MEASURE

STUD FINDER

HAMMER

PAINTBRUSH

PAINTER'S TAPE

DRILL

DRILL BITS

CAULKING GUN

5¹/₂" (14cm)

1 x 2" (2.5 x 5 cm) board

Using a doorframe as a guide, I designed the coat wall to be just about 5¹/₂ inches (14cm) deep to get the most storage and organization without impeding the walkway. (Before you get started with the installation, be sure to locate and mark the studs in your wall!)

First I attached bead board paneling, turned horizontally for a more modern look, with finishing nails down each groove and stud line. On the top and bottom of the paneling, I installed 1×2-inch (2.5×5cm) boards as shelf braces, nailing them to the paneling rather than the wall to help secure the paneling.

Next, I added the top shelf, which was a 1×6-inch (2.5×15cm) board, setting it flush to the wall and nailing into the 1×2-inch (2.5×5cm) shelf braces at the top and bottom of the paneling. I added a second shelf at the bottom of the paneling. I then installed a third shelf, braced with another 1×2-inch (2.5×5cm) board, centered between the top shelf and the ceiling and a fourth shelf centered between the bottom shelf and the floor.

Using 1×6-inch (2.5×15cm) boards again, I added the sides from the floor to the ceiling, nailing the sides into the shelves. At the floor, I cut and rounded the 1×6-inch (2.5×15cm) board to fit over the baseboard.

I caulked all the edges, shelves, and 1×2-inch (2.5×5cm) braces and painted everything with a primer after the caulk dried. I finished with an oil-based paint in a matte finish.

After the paint was dry, I added six coat/hat hooks across the top of the paneling, secured into the studs for extra strength, and installed seven smaller hooks to the underside of the top shelf. Then I filled the wall with baskets, buckets, and other storage pieces.

This is one area that gets lots of usage! For more how-to information and inspirational photos, visit thecreativityexchange.com/organizing-your-life.

after

THE MUDROOM

Make your own label!

1 **HOOKS AND LABELS**
Adding labels above the hooks helps family remember which hook is theirs.

2 **SMALL HOOKS**
You can never have too many hooks in the entryway. These smaller hooks are ideal for keeping track of keys.

3 **OPEN STORAGE**
Open storage below seating allows for additional storage of everyday items.

4 **CABINETS**
Using closed cabinets with shelving affords you the opportunity to corral items without the appearance of clutter.

◀ photo credit: Honey We're Home

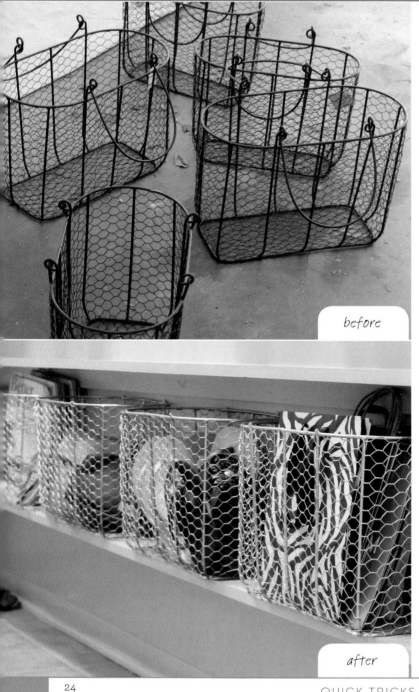

before

after

TRICK #1
SPRAY PAINT WIRE BASKETS TO MATCH YOUR DÉCOR

Can't find wire baskets to match your entryway décor? That's not a problem with this quick trick. Simply use spray primer and paint to change the color of mismatched wire storage baskets.

Prepare the baskets with a thin coat of spray primer, and allow it to dry. Then spray two thin coats of paint in your desired color, allowing the paint to dry in between coats.

Be sure to check out clearance sections for unpopular colors and great deals you can make over!

TRICK #2
COVER A COAT RACK WITH WALLPAPER

Coat hooks can be rather boring and blah. But you can easily dress up your coat or hat rack into something chic and pretty!

All you need to do is cover a piece of plywood, cut to your desired dimensions, with wallpaper before adding the hooks. If your wallpaper is self-pasting, simply dip it in water to activate the paste and smoothly cover the board. If your wallpaper does not have paste, use a wide paintbrush to apply a coat of wallpaper paste to the top and sides of the board and then adhere the paper and use a credit card to smooth out any air bubbles. Pull the wallpaper tight to the back side of the board, and secure with nails or staples. Let the wallpaper dry for a bit before adding the hooks, and secure the finished piece to the wall with toggle bolts so it's extra secure.

before

after

CHECKLIST 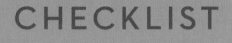 ENTRYWAY AND EXITS

notes

storage pieces

quick tricks

inspiration

AMANDACAROLINTERIORS.COM
HONEYWE'REHOME.BLOGSPOT.COM
DESIGNINDULGENCE.BLOGSPOT.COM
THECREATIVITYEXCHANGE.COM

tips

- Walls are the perfect place to install hooks for coats, bags, backpacks, hats, scarves, etc.

- Do you have an entryway table? What's under it? If nothing currently resides there, add a large basket to corral items such as shoes.

- Don't forget the corners! Use that overlooked area for narrow umbrella holders or coat racks.

- Pretty baskets on entryway tables are perfect for storing mail.

- Small decorative trays on tabletops can be both pretty and functional for corralling keys, change, and smaller items.

- Bins and larger baskets are a great way to store magazines and books that are dropped here.

- Assess your trouble spots. Look for items that tend to pile up around the entryway and exits to determine what items need a fix. If shoes are a problem, wrangle them with a large basket or a bench with built-in shoe storage. If magazines, mail, and other little things tend to litter the entryway table, place a large basket on the table and encourage your family to toss all those little things in it.

- A fresh coat of paint can transform an old dresser into a great entryway tabletop. As a bonus, the drawers can serve as additional storage.

- An old coat rack spray painted in a bright and bold color is a fun way to add a pop of color—and more storage.

KITCHEN

It's all too easy to have more kitchen tools, gadgets, and equipment than the drawer and cabinet space required to hold all those items. Therefore, maximizing all your potential kitchen space and sorting out duplicate items is essential for getting—and staying—organized in the kitchen.

Oftentimes, items are housed in the kitchen that aren't necessarily used in there—or aren't used often enough to warrant keeping them there. Floral vases, entertaining items, and large serving pieces only occasionally brought out and used can be stored in other areas of the home. Look to the dining room, storage cabinets in other rooms, and even closets to hold these items instead. Identifying and relocating those seldom-used items taking up space in your kitchen means more storage space for those pieces you do use often.

THE
KITCHEN

1 MICROWAVE PLACEMENT
Building the microwave into the cabinets and getting it up off the counter allows for more food prep area.

2 CABINETS
Cabinets that extend to the ceiling provide much-needed storage and no wasted space.

3 PANTRY
A separate, dedicated pantry area is ideal when planning the perfect kitchen.

4 ISLAND
An island serves multiple roles as an additional work surface or serving area, optional seating, and hidden storage below.

◀ photo credit: Donna Dotan Photography and cleandesignpartners.com

THE COUNTERTOP

1 FLAT BASKETS OR TRAYS

Large, flat baskets or trays are handy for catching little stuff often tossed on the counter. When you need the counter space, you can quickly and easily remove the tray.

2 GARDEN PLANTERS

A small garden planter provides a decorative piece in which to store soaps, scrubbing pads, etc.

3 SMALL BASKETS

Cooking oils and sprays can be neatly organized in a small basket with handles close to your oven. The handles make it easy to move your supplies around the kitchen when needed.

4 CANISTERS

Canisters should be a staple in any kitchen. Countless varieties are available, and they provide a simple solution for storing coffee, sugar, flour, etc.

CREATIVE
CABINET STORAGE

1 TIERED SERVING STANDS

Use multitiered serving stands to store rarely used holiday china or dishes vertically, in a small amount of space, in cabinets. (You might need to adjust short shelves if your stand is tall.) Then, when you need a piece or two, you can access them quickly. These stands also can be used to hold hors d'oeuvre or serving dishes on the table when entertaining, leaving more room on the tabletop for your guests' dishes.

2 CABINETS

Turn a kitchen cabinet into a decorative open storage cabinet for pretty pieces such as elegant glassware and crystal. This is especially handy for use when entertaining. Save time and space by setting up a drink area directly below the cabinet, and guests can grab their own glasses. Simply remove hinges, calk the holes, and paint.

3 EXPANDABLE WIRE SHELF RISERS

Expandable wire shelf risers give you an additional shelf and also create storage space below. You can nearly double the space you have available by maximizing the height of your cabinets.

4 SHOE SHELVES

Insert shoe shelving storage pieces traditionally used in closets in your larger cabinets for easy and inexpensive shelving. Use them to hold pots and pans, lids, and more.

1 **PLASTIC BINS**
These plastic bins are great for stacking and doubling your storage space. Use them to store fruit, seasoning packets, and other small items.

2 **BASKETS**
Use baskets and other storage containers in the pantry to house breads, snacks, and other frequently used items for quick access.

Add labels to plastic bins to help your family keep the pantry in order and see where everything goes.

3 **PLASTIC TOTES**
Multipurpose plastic totes can separate and store a wide variety of food and other kitchen items.

4 **WIRE STORAGE CART**
If you have a larger pantry, consider a wire storage cart. You can wheel it out when unpacking groceries or while you're cooking, and tuck it back in the pantry, out of the way, when you're done.

1 CLEAR CONTAINERS
Use clear storage containers so you can see what you have at a glance.

Labels are a great way to instantly identify what you need.

2 LABELS
Add pretty labels to help distinguish one baking ingredient from another.

3 MULTIPLE-SIZE CANISTERS
Use canisters of all sizes to store baking supplies (as well as other food items) and make the most of the space available.

4 TIN CANISTERS
Metal tins give you an additional option for storing baking supplies and hardware. And rather than buying them new, why not spray paint seasonal or mismatched tins you have on hand?

Printable Baking Labels

By organizing your baking ingredients, spices, and accessories together in one cabinet, you create a quick and easy baking station—which might encourage you to bake more! These fun and functional printable labels enable you to personalize all your baking supplies.

MATERIALS

8$\frac{1}{2}$×11-INCH
(21.5×28CM) LABEL
PAPER

TOOLS

PRINTER

PEN OR MARKER

SCISSORS

I've designed a few different sizes of labels to fit various-volume canisters. I've included bigger labels for those ingredients like flour and sugar you might store in larger quantities and, therefore, use larger containers. Other labels are smaller to fit those jars and canisters that hold less of an item.

All you need for these pretty printable labels is 8$\frac{1}{2}$×11-inch (21.5×28cm) sheets of label paper, your printer, a pen or marker, and scissors. I opted for 3M label paper with removable adhesive so I can take off the labels later if I want.

To use the printables, go to thecreativityexchange.com/organizing-your-life, and download the blank label template. Either print the blank labels on 8$\frac{1}{2}$×11-inch (21.5×28cm) label paper and write on them with a pen or marker, or fill in the labels on your computer using image-editing software and then print. Adhere the labels to your containers.

These lovely labels will make you smile each time you open your organized cabinet—and inspire you to keep it orderly! For more how-to information and inspirational photos, visit thecreativity-exchange.com/organizing-your-life.

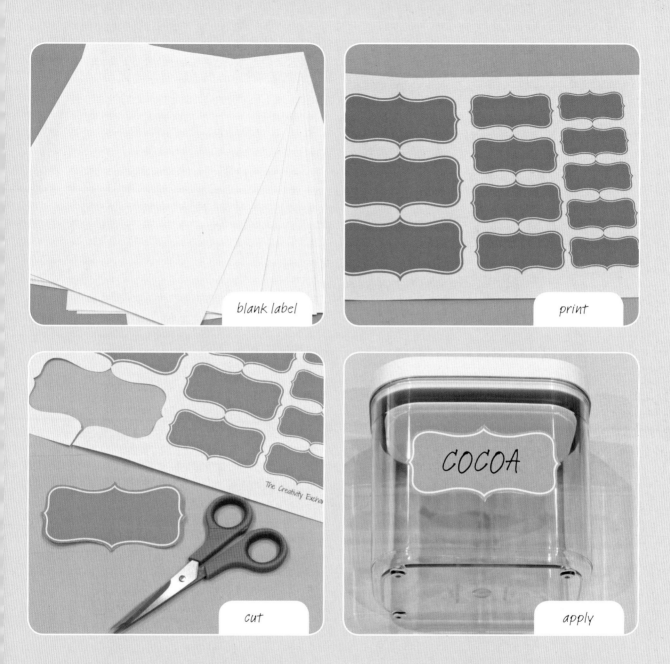

blank label

print

cut

apply

If you don't bake but you do, for example, love to can your garden crops, brew your own beer, or have another hobby that calls for a collection of items to be housed in your kitchen, you can use these labels to organize those things, too!

1 **WIDE CLEAR BINS**
Large, clear bins group like items to-gether and make the most of the limited refrigerator space you have available.

2 **NARROW CLEAR DRINK BINS**
Narrower bins can keep smaller items like drink pouches and boxes organized and house these items in a convenient space for kids to find.

3 **CAN HOLDERS**
Can holders double your storage opportunities by stacking cans. They also allow for quick access to canned beverages.

4 **SHELF RISERS**
Narrower bins can keep smaller items like drink pouches and boxes organized and house these items in a convenient space for kids to find.

DRAWERS

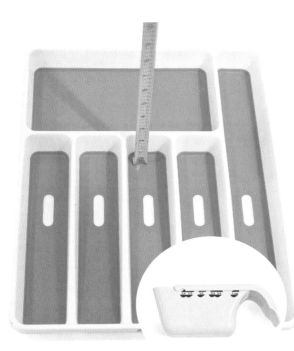

1 DEEP UTENSIL ORGANIZERS

Choose kitchen utensil organizers that are deep to hold the most implements. (Some utensil/silverware organizers are very shallow and waste a lot of space.) If you look for deeper drawer organizers, you can store almost double the number of items in a drawer.

Opt for all-in-one measuring pieces that offer multiple measurement options to eliminate the need for several bulky measuring pieces.

2 SPECIALIZED ORGANIZERS

Creating specialized drawers for housing serving utensils and entertaining pieces you don't use frequently frees up space in your more-often-used silverware and utensil drawers. Then, when you're entertaining, all your serving pieces are easy to find in one place.

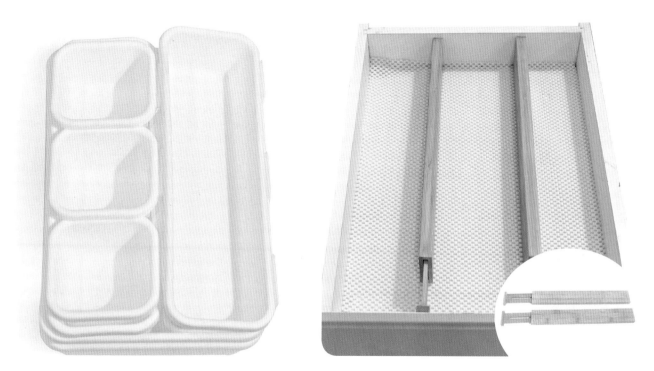

3 **CUSTOMIZABLE DRAWER ORGANIZERS**
Select drawer organizers that come in multiple shapes and sizes and stack and nest to make the most of limited drawer space.

4 **EXPANDABLE DRAWER INSERTS**
Expandable drawer inserts enable you to customize your drawer storage options by creating specifically sized compartments to hold just what you need to hold.

BOOKSHELF STORAGE

Don't waste space! Use the top of the bookshelf for large or awkward-size platters no one knows what to do with.

1 BOOKSHELVES

If you have the room, add a narrow book-shelf in your kitchen for more storage and décor opportunities.

2 COOKBOOK STORAGE

What better place than a bookshelf to store all your cookbooks or display some of your favorites? Plus, this keeps them within reach for easy access but off your countertop.

Tuck small plate or frame holders into bookshelves to dress up your stacked dishes.

3 SPACE-SAVING STACKS

Stacking dinnerware allows numerous dishes to fit neatly into a small space. This also enables you to show off some of your prettier pieces rather than close them behind cabinet doors.

4 ADDITIONAL HIDDEN STORAGE

Consider adding doors on the lower half of your bookshelves to increase the amount of hidden, closed-door storage in your kitchen. Use this area to store tablecloths, napkins, and other related items.

TRICK #1
CREATE A KITCHEN COMMAND CENTER

An easy way to keep your kitchen counters free of the clutter they tend to accumulate is to turn a cabinet into a hidden kitchen command center. By creating a mini-office in a kitchen cabinet, you can group all your office supplies and daily-use items in one easy-to-access spot, off the counter and tucked away behind closed doors. Use drawer organizers to hold paper, note cards, and envelopes in the front, and stack office trays in the back to hold notebooks, phone books, and other larger items. Adhere corkboard to the insides of the doors for to pin up notes, to-do lists, invitations, and more.

TRICK #2
REPAINT OLD COOKIE TINS FOR STYLISH STORAGE

Cookie tins are often exchanged during the holidays, filled with cookies, candies, and other treats. But after the holidays, you're left with a bunch of random, mismatched tins. Repurpose these tins into pretty, coordinated storage pieces with a little spray paint. First spray your tins with a thin coat of spray primer and allow to completely dry. Next, moving quickly and from a distance of at least 2 feet (.5m) away, spray on a thin coat of your desired color paint, just enough to completely cover the tin. Allow the paint to dry overnight before putting on the lid.

CHECKLIST

KITCHEN

notes

storage pieces

quick tricks

inspiration

CLEANDESIGNPARTERS.COM
DONNA DOTAN PHOTOGRAPHY
THECREATIVITYEXCHANGE.COM

tips

- The back sides of cabinet doors are ideal for holding hooks, over-the-door baskets, or hanging spice racks.

- Maximize drawer space by buying deep and expandable utensil organizers that fit the entire width and depth of your drawers.

- Blank kitchen walls can house floor-to-ceiling furniture such as a bookshelf that creates additional kitchen storage for serving pieces, cookbooks, and more.

- Free up additional pantry space by pulling out your baking ingredients and spices separately in a nearby cabinet.

- Use a plastic tub to hold duplicates of cooking utensils and rarely used gadgets, and store them in a cabinet to unclutter your utensil drawer.

- Use baskets or plastic tubs to stack muffin and cake pans vertically so you can grab the pan you need quickly and easily.

- Assess your trouble spots. Look at cabinets that give you the most problems and determine if you need to remove items and come up with creative storage solutions within the cabinets. For instance, if your cookie sheet/baking pan cabinet is always a mess, consider removing a shelf to stack items vertically to keep the cabinet in order. If your problem cabinet is the pots and pans cabinet, consider incorporating shoe shelving for additional organization.

- Transform an old china cabinet, hutch, or bookshelf into a beautiful open storage piece in your kitchen by removing the upper doors and updating it with a fresh coat of paint.

- Use extra baskets and plastic storage tubs and bins in the pantry to separate and organize ingredients and supplies.

DINING ROOM

The dining room can be one of the least-often used rooms in your home, with the least amount of furniture, which makes it perfect for creating additional organized storage. With all the multipurpose storage furniture pieces available today, you can really get creative when choosing storage in the dining room. For example, a console or sofa table can be used as a food buffet and still allow for hidden storage below.

In this section, you see that the dining room is the perfect space in which to organize seldom-used kitchen items such as large serving and entertaining pieces, holiday dishes, and surplus dishes and glassware. But storage here isn't limited to kitchen items. Use the organizing opportunities in the dining room for anything you need.

◀ photo credit: Katherine Scheele Photography

DINING ROOM STORAGE

1   **HIDDEN CABINET/BUFFET STORAGE**
A cabinet is a great way to store china and glass-ware. You also can make use of the top of the cabi-net to for pretty storage and décor.

2   **FURNITURE WITH DRAWERS**
Look for furniture pieces that can do double-duty with drawer space on top and open storage below for deep baskets. Tuck in extra dinnerware, linens, or larger serving pieces in these hidden-away spots.

▲ photo credit: Amanda Carol Interiors

▲ photo credit: Kirkland's

3 **DRESSER/CONSOLE TABLE**
An old dresser (minus a drawer or two) in the dining room can make a great bar or tabletop. Drawers add much-needed storage for items ranging from plates to games.

4 **OPEN SHELVING PIECES**
Opening shelving can be used to hold baskets and decorative storage pieces out in the open. And when you're entertaining, you can serve food or drinks from these pieces, making more room on your tabletop or in your kitchen for other items.

 photo credit: evolutionofstyleblog.blogspot.com

▲ photo credit: Kirkland's

1 **STACK DISHES**
Maximize space in the buffet (or even in your kitchen cabinets) by grouping and stacking like items.

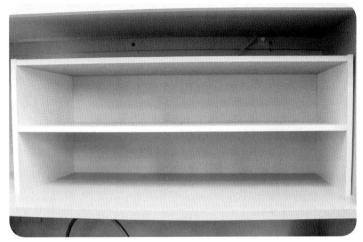

2 **SHOE SHELVING**
Inexpensive premade shoe shelving units meant for closets can create an additional layer of shelving in larger cabinets, giving you quick access to their contents.

3 **BASKETS**
Baskets are a great way to store small items and can be pulled out for quick and easy access.

4 **TRAYS**
Trays are perfect to use atop a buffet because they can corral decorative items and then be moved off the buffet easily when you're ready to serve food or drinks.

Hidden-Storage Buffet

The dining room often presents a unique challenge. Usually, so much of the room is taken up by the table and chairs, even when they're not in use, not much space is left for other furniture. Add guests around your table, and your room shrinks even more. But having a place to store your good china or larger or less frequently used serving dishes in this room is helpful—and frees up space in your kitchen. This DIY buffet is only 16 inches (40.5cm) wide, doesn't interfere with the walking space around the table, and provides lots of hidden storage.

MATERIALS

4×8-FOOT (1.25×2.5M) SHEETS OF 1-INCH (2.5CM) THICK PLYWOOD

1×6-INCH (2.5×15CM) BOARDS

SHEETS OF MDF BOARD

NAILS

FINISHING TRIM

½-INCH (1.25CM) THICK TRIM, ROUNDED ON ONE EDGE

CAULK

PAINT

HINGES

TOOLS

PENCIL

TAPE MEASURE

SAW

HAMMER

CAULKING GUN

PAINTBRUSH

SCREWDRIVER

If you attempt this project, be sure you use extra-sturdy materials that will hold up to the weight of your dishes and not buckle or break.

I built the frame using sheets of 1-inch (2.5cm) thick plywood cut to 15×34¾ inches (38×88.25cm) for the two sides and 15×83½ inches (38×212cm) for the bottom and middle shelves. Assembly was quick and easy using nails.

I added a 1×6-inch (2.5×15cm) board under the middle of the bottom shelf for reinforcement.

Then I cut two 15×15-inch (38×38cm) pieces and attached them between each shelf, in the center, for reinforcement as well as two more reinforcement 1×6-inch (2.5×15cm) boards evenly spaced under the bottom shelf.

I cut the top of the buffet to 15×85½ (38×217cm)—2 inches (5cm) longer than the shelves because it fit over the tops of the side pieces. I cut another piece 1×3¾ inches (2.5×9.5cm) and added it to the front bottom base to hide the reinforcements there.

I set the buffet in the dining room and trimmed the front edges and the center support with 1×3-inch (2.5×7.5cm) boards.

I cut the 20⅝×31¼-inch (52.5×79.25cm) doors from a sheet of MDF so they wouldn't warp and attached them to the buffet with hinges. I added a thin piece of ½-inch (1.25cm) trim, rounded on one edge, to finish the end of the buffet. I then caulked and painted the piece.

I'm so excited to have this buffet in my dining room to hold all my china and serving pieces—and also have a long surface to use when I entertain. You could make your own buffet a different size depending on how much space you have to work with and your organizational needs. For more how-to information and inspirational photos, visit thecreativityexchange.com/organizing-your-life.

1 **TIERED CART**
A tiered cart can be easily turned into a bar/beverage cart. It's an inexpensive way to organize barware and easy to roll out when you're entertaining.

2 **GLASSWARE BASKET**
Rather than storing glassware plainly on the shelf, add a pretty basket to keep stem ware and other glasses organized. (This also helps you carry these breakable items to and from the kitchen during cleanup.)

3 **STORAGE CONTAINERS**
Opt for fun and colorful baskets, bins, and other containers when storing bar or beverage accessories. These containers can go from the refrigerator to the cart with little hassle.

 photo credit: dreamgreendiy.com

4 **TOP SHELF**
Make the most of this area to hold often-used items, serve as your drink-mixing sufrace, showcase your decorative glassware, and free up valuable kitchen cabinet space.

TRICK #1

REPURPOSE UNUSED FURNITURE AROUND THE HOUSE

Convert a wide dresser into a tabletop buffet from which to serve food and drinks when entertaining. Store linens, extra china or seldom-used entertaining dishes, and flatware in the drawers.

▲ photo credit: Amanda Carol Interiors

TRICK #2
SPRAY PAINT TIERED SERVING PIECES

Maximize the top of a buffet or side table when entertaining by using tiered serving pieces. You often can find these serving solutions in the clearance aisle of home stores. A quick coat of matching spray paint on all of them, and they look like they were meant to go together.

CHECKLIST

DINING ROOM

notes

storage pieces

quick tricks

inspiration

AMANDACAROLINTERIORS.COM
DREAMGREENDIY.COM
EVOLUTIONOFSTYLEBLOG.BLOGSPOT.COM
KIRKLAND'S
THECREATIVITYEXCHANGE.COM

tips

- Blank walls or corners are perfect for closed cabinet storage furniture pieces that can be used to hold virtually anything.

- Install inexpensive floating shelves to create additional on-the-wall storage for pretty glassware, serving pieces, and china.

- Upholstered storage benches are great dining room dual-purpose pieces. They offer both seating and organizing opportunities.

- Use baskets or decorative bins on open shelving to store linens, extra dishes, or serving pieces.

- Make ample use of stackable bins to contain the little stuff inside closed storage furniture.

- Small console tables or tiered bar/beverage carts are ideal for organizing bar accessories and glassware. As a bonus, they can serve as a beverage serving area when you're entertaining.

- Assess your trouble spots. Take a close look at what clutter frequently tends to end up in the dining room and on the dining room table specifically. If your table is cluttered with mail, bags, keys, and other small items, consider creating storage solutions in your entryway to corral these things. For other clutter, place a large tray or basket on the table to catch stray items. You can then grab the tray or basket and quickly and easily take it away to clear the table.

- Use an old dresser as a buffet on the top, and utilize the drawers below for storage. Line the drawers with felt, and house old china, silver, and antique serving pieces inside.

- Dress up traditional narrow bookshelves for the dining room by attaching two together and adding molding around the edges.

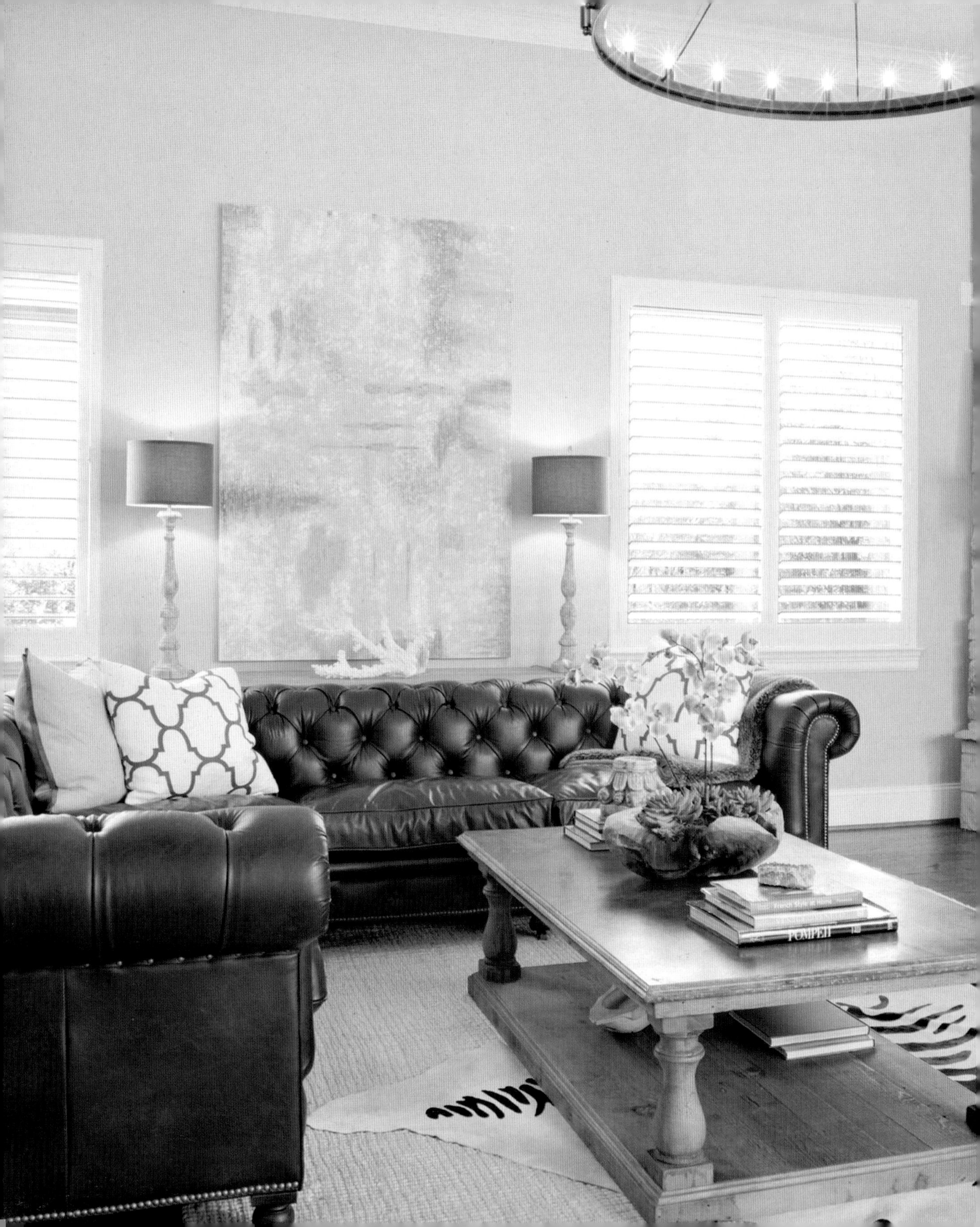
POMPEII

LIVING AND FAMILY ROOMS

The living room or family room is often the most used space in the home. By incorporating storage pieces such as baskets, bins, and trays out in the open, rather than closed away where they can be easily forgotten, you increase the chances of keeping this space organized.

But don't rule out closed storage pieces altogether. Another key to getting—and keeping—the living room/family room organized is to choose furniture pieces that allow for additional storage. Today, you can find many kinds of stylish yet functional furniture options. Choosing these pieces—and implementing open storage as well—can make a major impact on organization in these busy rooms.

◄ photo credit: Amanda Carol Interiors

Large trays work well for keeping magazines or books organized.

Lidded baskets are ideal for containing clutter out of sight.

1 **BASKETS AND TRAYS**
Use baskets and trays liberally through-out this room to contain the small stuff that seems to accumulate here, such as magazines, photos, remote controls, etc.

2 **COFFEE TABLES**
Opt for a coffee table that offers twice the storage with a large tabletop and an extra shelf below.

3 **ARMOIRES/BOOKSHELVES**
You can never have too many ar-moires or bookshelves in your house. These versatile pieces allow for more much-needed hidden storage. Don't forget to utilize the top of the storage piece as well.

4 **END TABLES**
End tables with shelves or drawers give you more room to organize baskets, bins, and other items that often linger around the living area. Multitiered tables can double or triple the amount of usable space.

Separating the little stuff with baskets and bins can help keep everything in order and still give you quick access to the items inside.

1 BOOKSHELVES/ARMOIRES

Bookshelves and armoires neatly house all the accessories that can accompany a TV and provide extra organizing o9pportunities on the other shelves. Best of all, when the armoire doors are closed, all the electronic elements are out of sight.

2 SHELVES AND DRAWERS

Furniture pieces that contain shelves and drawers easily hold baskets in which you can organize movies and games.

3 PLANT URNS

Get creative and use decorative plant urns to store card games, remotes, or other small items. These come in a variety of shapes and sizes.

4 CABINET DOORS

Adding cabinet doors to a bookshelf allows you to close off some of the electronic accessory, movie, and game clutter.

ORGANIZING
ELECTRONIC CORDS

1 OUTLET HUBS

Organizing cords and chargers is so much easier with all-in-one multipurpose outlet hubs that have USB plugs, electrical outlets, built-in holders for your charging electronic devices, and even a place to wrap charge cords so they don't get tangled.

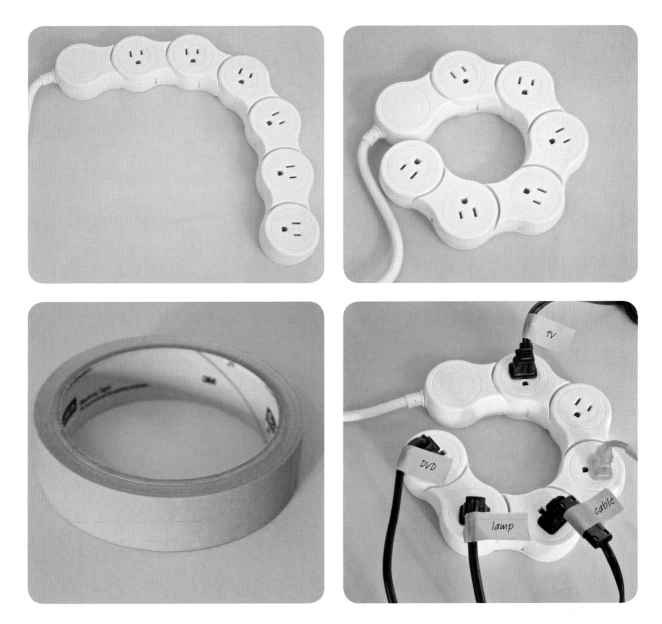

2 POWER STRIPS

An easy way to keep cords organized and prevent them from getting tangled is to use flexible power strips you can stretch and bend to fit the space available.

When plugging multiple items into a power strip, make identification simple by labeling each cord. Fold a small strip of masking or painter's tape over the cord and squeeze the sticky sides together. Write what item the cord belongs to at the base of the tape, and you'll never unplug the wrong thing again.

BOOKSHELVES

1   BUILT-INS OR MULTIPLE BOOKSHELVES

By creating custom built-ins or connecting multiple premade bookshelves, you can create an eye-catching wall storage unit.

2   BASKETS AND BINS

Adding baskets and bins to your shelving allows you to neatly store your books, magazines, games, DVDs, and more.

3   GLASS JARS

Large glass jars are perfect for holding card, dice, and other games. They're neatly organized and you can find at a glance what you're looking for.

Wall Bookshelf/ Entertainment Center

Almost any type of furniture can help you get a room organized, but imagine designing and building your own personalized pieces to hold exactly what you want them to hold! With a little creativity, an afternoon or more of labor, and some inexpensive materials, you can craft a custom wall bookshelf or entertainment center to fit just about whatever space you have available.

MATERIALS

12-INCH (30CM) SHELVING BOARDS

1×2-INCH (2.5×5CM) BOARDS

SCREWS

PAINT

TOOLS

PENCIL

TAPE MEASURE

STUD FINDER

SAW

DRILL

DRILL BITS

PAINTBRUSH

PAINTER'S TAPE

Before you get started with the installation, be sure to locate and mark the studs in your wall.

The key to this project is planning. You need to carefully evaluate your space and just as carefully design what you want your bookshelves or entertainment center to look like.

For example, if you base your design on using standard, 12-inch (30cm) shelving boards, you can lower both labor and costs because you don't have to cut the wood narrower. And to save even more money, consider using the wall upon which you're building your shelves as the backing of the cabinets instead of using more wood there. You can either leave the wall the original paint color or paint it the same color as the shelving unit.

After you've designed your bookshelf or entertainment center, cut your boards to the required lengths specified in your design. Then begin installation. It's easiest to assemble your shelves on the floor first and then attach the whole frame to the wall, being sure to screw into studs for strength and support.

DO IT YOURSELF

1x2-inch (2.5x5cm) support boards

For extra security and stabilization, you can attach 1×2-inch (2.5×5cm) boards horizontally just below the larger shelves. Screw these supports into the wall studs and then secure the shelves to the support by screwing down into the shelf and the support.

Arrange and install individual shelves within the bookshelves as you like, and give it a coat of paint. Fill with books, baskets, bins, or whatever you have planned for your new bookshelves or entertainment center! For more how-to information and inspirational photos, visit thecreativityexchange.com/organizing-your-life.

after

1 TRAYS

Shallow trays are excellent for holding smaller items without blocking anyone's view. Plus, you can pick up and move them easily when you need more space.

2 BASKETS

Decorative baskets are useful in any room of the house and are ideal both for longer-term storage and for items used on a daily basis. Spruce up any basket easily by adding a liner, and opt for baskets with handles when you can.

3 BOXES

Decorative boxes come in all shapes, sizes, and styles. Lidded boxes make fantastic storage space for items less frequently used. You also can easily group and stack boxes when needed.

4 COFFEE TABLES

Dual-purpose coffee tables with additional storage underneath can really help organize the little stuff. Adding baskets or bins below to catch the clutter for quick and easy cleanup.

◀ photo credit: Amanda Carol Interiors and Lauren Giles

HIDDEN STORAGE

1 STORAGE OTTOMANS

Storage ottomans make excellent du-al-purpose pieces for the living room. Use them as a coffee table on the top, adding a large shallow tray for a hard tabletop surface if you like, and store games, blankets, extra pillows, etc. below.

2 STORAGE BENCHES

Storage benches offer additional seating areas in the living areas, especially along blank or short walls or under windows. Benches with space below for baskets or drawers mean even more storage for books, games, toys, etc.

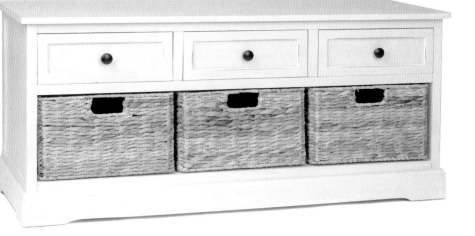

▲ photo credit: Kirkland's

3   STORAGE CHESTS WITH DRAWERS

Shallow chests of drawers are ideal for narrow walkways in the living area. They don't take up a lot of room but still provide organizing surfaces for baskets and trays on top and hidden storage in the drawers below.

4   MULTIPURPOSE STORAGE CHESTS

Storage pieces with multiple drawers, doors, and bins offer versatile organizing opportunities above and below.

▲ photo credit: Kirkland's

TRICK #1
SECURE REMOTES AND GAME CONTROLLERS INSIDE CABINET DOORS

Never lose a remote or game controller again! Adhere them to the inside of entertainment center or armoire doors with hook-and-loop tape, and you'll always know where to find them.

TRICK #2
REPURPOSE A SILVERWARE CADDY FOR REMOTES AND PENS

Baskets or boxes meant to be used in one room can be repurposed for use in other rooms. This silverware caddy comes out of the kitchen and into the living room to hold remotes, reading glasses, pens and paper, and more.

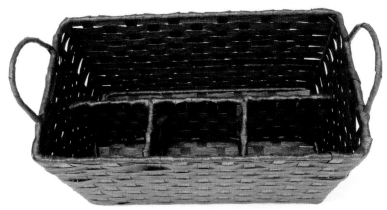

CHECKLIST

LIVING AND FAMILY ROOMS

notes

storage pieces

quick tricks

inspiration

AMANDACAROLINTERIORS.COM
KIRKLAND'S
THECREATIVITYEXCHANGE.COM

tips

- Choose furniture pieces that create the maximum amount of storage for an area. A tall bookshelf can provide two or three times as much storage as a small table or chest in the same area.

- Add a narrow sofa table with top and bottom shelving behind the sofa for additional organized storage.

- Blank walls or corners are the perfect spot for closed cabinet storage furniture pieces. These can hold virtually anything.

- Switch out a couple decorative items on shelves with storage baskets. You'll be surprised how this simple change can go a long way toward keeping rooms organized.

- Place decorative garden urns on the hearth or on tabletops to corral books, magazines, and other little items.

- Set large baskets next to the sofa or a chair, and encourage their use as catch-alls to keep the area free of clutter.

- Assess your trouble spots. Take a close look at the items in your living room/family room that frequently find their way to the coffee table or identify other areas of disarray. For example, if games, DVDs, and books tend to pile up, consider storing them in cabinets and bookshelves in large boxes or baskets with side handles so you can pull out the boxes or baskets, grab what you want, and put the box or basket back rather than pulling out several at a time.

- Spray paint old trays and wooden boxes in fun colors to help organize the coffee table, end tables, or bookshelves.

- Utilize an old wardrobe or armoire for storage in the living room. These pieces are tall and really maximize the space available. They're ideal for storing extra blankets, pillows, and linens.

BATHROOMS

Bathrooms can be challenging rooms to organize because of all the soaps, lotions, cosmetics, linens, and other items commonly housed here. But your options for organizing are plentiful here, too. Many creative storage and organizing products are available, as are hidden areas of unused space in this room. The key to getting organized is to identify the areas of wasted space in your bathroom and capitalize on them with smart storage solutions.

Regular purging is also key for organizing the bathroom. Tossing old makeup, medicine, and other bathroom products you no longer use instantly frees drawer and cabinet space. Keeping a plastic bin under the sink for housing rarely used items is a great way to make more room in drawers and cabinets for the things you and your family use daily.

◀ photo credit: Heather Garrett Designs

1   VANITIES

The vanity you choose can help eliminate clutter in and around the bathroom. Choose a vanity with plenty of counter and drawer space if you can, rather than a small pedestal sink with no storage. Within the drawers, be sure to make the most of the space available with trays, bins, partitions, etc.

2   TIP-OUT CABINETS/HAMPERS

A tilt-out cabinet allows you to conveniently hide your laundry or bathroom linens under the sink rather than taking up space in a closet.

Bathroom storage pieces come in multiple sizes, shapes, and arrangements of shelves. They're perfect for storing bath products and other small items.

3   GARDEN STOOLS

Not just for outside, a garden stool makes a pretty bathroom accent piece. They're handy for small-space seating and can be used to hold extra towels or a basket of bath products.

◀ photo credit: Heather Garrett Designs

1 **CERAMIC POTS/URNS**
Found at any garden center, ceramic pots and urns are excellent for storing brushes, combs, and other beauty products.

2 **TRAYS**
Pretty trays help keep the bathroom countertop looking clean and organized and can group a multitude of loose items.

3 **DECORATIVE PIECES**
Easily repurpose items you love. For example, this glass candy dish works well for storing hand towels. Baskets are another alternative for organizing towels. Roll or fold towels, and tuck them neatly into any basket.

4 **SMALL GLASS CONTAINERS**
Small, clear glass containers are ideal for storing cotton balls, cotton swabs, and soaps.

1 **HANDLED BASKETS**
Narrow baskets are useful for storing bath products out of the way. The handles make them easy to grab and go with you to the shower or tub.

2 **ADJUSTABLE SHELVING**
If your cabinet allows for adjustable shelving, adjust it! Raise or lower shelves to make the most of the space you have and fit the specific storage containers you want to use there.

3 **CLEAR PLASTIC TRAYS**
These see-through trays can store lots of little stuff used in the bathroom. Look for divided trays to further organize bath products and other items.

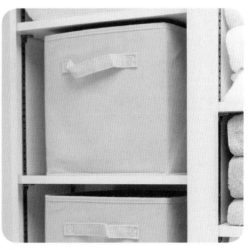

4 **CLOTH BINS**
Cloth bins are a necessity in the linen cabinet. Opt for bins as tall as possible to fit your cabinet to house a multitude of items neatly out of sight.

1 **PLASTIC DRAWER ORGANIZERS**
These organizers are ideal for keeping medicines visible and in order.

2 **CLEAR BOXES AND BINS**
These clear organizers are ideal for holding those items you and your family use frequently.

3 **STACKABLE BINS**
Stackable bins are a great option for storing items vertically in spots where you don't have a lot of space to spare.

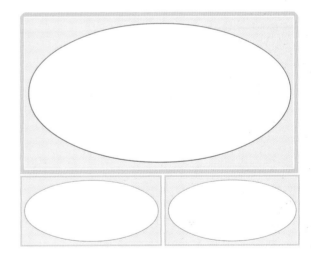

4 **PRINTABLE LABELS**
Clean and clear labels help you see at a glance what you have and where it's located. Labeling your content makes finding your items easier later on.

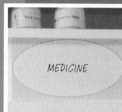

MEDICINE

Printable Bathroom Labels

I'm a big fan of labels. Especially in a small space like the bathroom cabinet, where you have lots of bins, baskets, trays, and other storage containers, it's easy to overlook what you have. By labeling what's in all those storage containers, you can save time when you're looking for something specific.

MATERIALS

8$\frac{1}{2}$×11-INCH
(21.5×28CM) LABEL
PAPER

TOOLS

PRINTER

PEN OR MARKER

SCISSORS

All you need for these printable labels is 8$\frac{1}{2}$×11-inch (21.5×28cm) sheets of label paper, your printer, a pen or marker, and scissors.

To create the labels, go to thecreativityexchange.com/organizing-your-life, and download the blank label template. Either print the blank labels on 8$\frac{1}{2}$×11-inch (21.5×28cm) label paper and write on them with a pen or marker, or fill in the labels on your computer using image-editing software and then print. Adhere the labels to your containers, and you're done!

For more how-to information and inspirational photos, visit thecreativityexchange.com/organizing-your-life.

These labels would work great elsewhere, too. Try them in a closet, your child's room, the pantry, or the laundry room.

MAKEUP DRAWERS

1 PLASTIC DESK ORGANIZERS

Repurpose inexpensive desk drawer organizers in your makeup drawer! These handy organizers hold all sizes and shapes of makeup containers and are easy to trim to fit any drawer. Use several next to each other if you have room.

2 ORGANIZE WITH COLOR

For easy organization and identification, spray paint desk drawer organizers in different colors to hold makeup for different family members.

Storing your brushes together makes them easier to find.

3 COMPARTMENTS

The various sizes and shapes of the organizer's compartments make it easier to keep like items together.

Spray Painted Drawer Organizers

Every girl needs a little pop of fun in her makeup cabinet, jewelry box, or desk drawer. This is a super simple and inexpensive project to do just that—and keep all your drawers tidy and organized! (These fun and colorful organizers work for guys' stuff, too, of course!)

MATERIALS

DESK DRAWER ORGANIZING TRAYS

SPRAY PAINT

SPRAY PRIMER SPECIFICALLY FOR USE ON PLASTIC

TOOLS

NONE

You certainly can go out and buy colorful, prettily designed, and more expensive organizing containers, but here's a little secret I've discovered: desk drawer organizing trays work just as well, and they're easy to customize to match your colors and décor! What's more, they're usually much less expensive than the designer containers, and you can find them in nearly any office supply store or even drug store. The trays are often designed in a few different ways, with compartments for corralling smaller and larger items alike, making them perfect for organizing almost anything—makeup, jewelry, hair accessories, small kitchen gadgets, office supplies, and even nuts and bolts in the garage.

The only potential downfall to these trays is their color. Usually black, they're not all that nice to look at (unless black is your color!). That's where spray paint comes in. With very little work, you can open your drawers or cabinets and smile when you see these fun and colorful organizers keeping all your stuff in place.

The best way to spray paint plastic and guarantee it won't scratch off is to use a primer specifically made for use on plastic. The trick when using plastic primer is to spray on *two* coats and allow at least 20 minutes between each coat. Then, *you must wait at least 1 hour* after the second coat before painting.

In a well-ventilated area, place your desk trays on a drop cloth, newspaper, or another surface over which you can spray paint. Spray on two coats of the plastic primer, allowing the requisite time between each application. When you're ready to paint, spray a light coat of color over the trays and let dry for about 20 minutes.

Less is more when it comes to spraying plastic, so if you need to apply another coat of color, do so *lightly*. Let your trays dry at least 24 to 48 hours to allow for the paint to fully set. For more information, visit thecreativityexchange.com/organizing-your-life.

before

after-gold

after-blue

Don't limit yourself to colors. Try metallic spray paint, too!

1 STACKABLES

Stackable plastic bins help keep the many items located in a child's bathroom in one central location. It also teaches them that every item has a place other than on the countertop.

2 TOY ORGANIZERS

Every child's bathroom needs something to corral bath toys. Opt for a large plastic bin or tub, and store it under the sink and out of sight. Be sure to pick one that contains holes so the wet toys can drain after use.

3 DRAWER ORGANIZERS

You can't have too many drawer organizers in your house. Silverware and kitchen utensil organizers are a great way to organize items in vanity drawers. Spray paint them in fun, coordinating colors!

◀ photo credit: Jenna Buck Gross

Creative Drawer Liners

If you have loads of large gift bags taking up space in a drawer or closet, why not repurpose them as pretty drawer liners? With this project, you can add a pop of color and fun to your drawers—and recycle, too!

MATERIALS

LARGE PAPER
GIFT BAGS WITH A
GLOSSY FINISH

GLUE DOTS OR
DOUBLE-SIDED TAPE

TOOLS

TAPE MEASURE

RULER

SCISSORS

1. Choose a bag that has a glossy finish for easier cleanup. And opt for one large enough to cover the entire surface of your drawer so you don't have to use the folded edges. (The creases won't be pretty.)

2. Measure the inside of your drawer to get the exact width and length.

3. Flatten the gift bag, and measure and mark your drawer measurements. Use a ruler to draw a line on which you can cut to be sure the edges are straight.

4. Cut the bag on the lines you drew.

5. Place glue dots or double-sided tape in the corners of the drawer and at various spots around the edges of the drawer.

6. Add the recycled drawer liner, and press down to secure.

This fun project isn't limited to a child's bathroom; feel free to use this idea anywhere in your house! For more information, visit thecreativityexchange.com/organizing-your-life.

CREATIVE DRAWER LINERS

TRICK #1
RECYCLE VOTIVE CANDLEHOLDERS AS BATHROOM STORAGE

I encourage you to get creative when thinking about containers in which you can store items. For example, if you have several unused glass candleholders, repurpose them as bathroom storage containers. If the candleholders still have candle wax in the bottom, pop them into the freezer for a couple hours. As the wax freezes, it condenses. You might be able to wiggle it out using your fingers, or you might have to carefully chip it out using a butter knife. Remove any remaining wax residue from the sides with a quick trip through the dishwasher. Use these pretty little containers for holding cotton swabs, makeup removers, and more.

TRICK #2
INSTALL HOOKS FOR TOWELS

In busy bathrooms—children's or otherwise—towels are sometimes hurridly tossed on the floor. To help everyone remember to hang their towels, it helps to have a dedicated towel rack that's easy to see and, therefore, remember to use. To help your childen remember to hang their towels, install a row of hooks in their bathroom, allowing a specific hook for each child and maybe an extra one if you have room. Double hooks provide even more storage for towels, robes, or small buckets that hold kids' bath products.

▲ photo credit: evolutionofstyleblog.blogspot.com

CHECKLIST BATHROOMS

notes

storage pieces

quick tricks

inspiration

HEATHERGARRETTDESIGN.COM
EVOLUTIONOFSTYLEBLOG.BLOGSPOT.COM
COLORDRUNK.BLOGSPOT.COM
THECREATIVITYEXCHANGE.COM

tips

- Install additional towel racks on the wall behind the bathroom door. Consider adding two towel racks, one lower and the other higher, for additional towel storage.

- Utilize the corners of the bathroom for small glass or metal multitiered bathroom shelving to hold towels and bath products.

- Make use of the wall space over towel racks and toilets for additional storage or wall cabinets.

- Hang floating shelves next to the vanity and bathtub area to create additional storage adjacent to where products are used the most.

- Tuck shoe shelving in the cabinets under the sink for a quick and easy way to create extra shelving and maximize the height of this space.

- Set a basket in a corner next to the toilet to store extra toilet paper, which frees up space in cabinets for other items.

- Assess your trouble spots. Look at the cabinets that give you the most problems in the bathroom and determine if you need to purge items or find better storage options. If you have adjustable shelving, maximize the height of the shelves to accommodate the height of the items you're storing.

- Use garden urns and glass candleholders for a pretty and functional way to store bath products and supplies on the top of the vanity and on shelves.

- Paint an old dresser or nightstand with a high-gloss paint to protect it from moisture, and use it for an additional organizing surface on top and storage in the drawers below.

LAUNDRY ROOM

Even though laundry rooms vary in size and style from home to home, the key to getting—and staying—organized here remains the same: maximizing every area you have available and choosing functional storage pieces that fit with how you and your family use the laundry space.

In this section, you see three very different laundry spaces, each loaded with creative organizing ideas and examples of taking full advantage of the space available. All three also boast functional and creative ways of storing supplies and areas for folding and hanging clothes. With a few smart strategies, you, too, can have an organized laundry room.

◄ photo credit: sandandsisal.com

1 BASKETS FOR STORAGE

Smaller baskets or bins with handles make perfect containers in the laundry room. They provide additional storage and easy access for fabric softeners, stain-removal products, and other laundry items.

2 LONG SHELVING FOR LAUNDRY BASKETS

If you have room for longer shelving, it's worth adding to store laundry baskets below and give you a folding area above. Either wood or wire shelving would work.

Use clear glass apothecary jars and bottles to hold detergent, fabric softener, and more.

3 HOOKS

Hooks in your laundry room enable to hang many items that would otherwise clutter the top of your washer and dryer, folding surface, shelves, etc.

4 SHELVES

Remember to put any and all wasted wall space to use. Shelving is simple to install and offers an easy-access area for storing laundry detergent and other supplies.

◀ photo credit: sandandsisal.com

SMALL LAUNDRY SPACES

1 OVERHEAD CABINETS

Even the smallest laundry spaces can be creatively transformed to optimize organizational opportunities. This laundry room, which was once a closet, was renovated into a functional and workable space. By adding open or closed cabinets overhead, you maximize the space and create additional hidden storage.

2 CLOSET RODS

Add hanging rods designed for closets in overhead areas in your laundry room to give you a spot to hang clean clothes.

3 FOLDING AREA

Install a countertop on top of front-loading washers and dryers to create a level folding and laundry preparation space.

◀ photo credit: Donna Dotan Photography and cleandesignpartners.com

CREATIVE STORAGE IDEAS

1 **ROLLING HAMPERS**
Large laundry hampers on wheels enable you to roll in dirty laundry from another room (saving space in your laundry room) and then roll out the clean, folded laundry to be put away.

2 **HANGING AREAS**
Install wire shelving systems in the wasted space above your washer and dryer to hold out-of-season clothes or other items. Opt for the kind of shelving that has a hanging rod built in below you can use to hang clean clothes.

3 **BASKETS AND BINS**
As in all other rooms in your house, employ baskets and bins in your laundry room, too. Make the most of your available space by measuring and adjusting your shelves as needed to fit the storage containers you want to use.

4 **JARS AND BUCKETS**
Use lots of small jars and even buckets to hold cleaning supplies, clothespins, clips, and other little laundry items. Or dedicate one for collecting the spare change, keys, and other items commonly forgotten in pants pockets.

Easy Wire Shelving Systems

Wire shelving systems enable you to create custom organization and storage solutions. They're often easy to install, and they're very designed to be very customizable to the space you have to work with, whether that's the laundry room, kitchen pantry, linen closet, etc. Even better, they're often less expensive than other storage systems.

MATERIALS

WIRE SHELVING SYSTEM COMPONENTS— UPRIGHTS, BRAC- ES, BRACKETS, SHELVES, HANGING RODS, HOOKS, ETC.

TOOLS

TOOLS SPECIFIED BY SHELVING SYS- TEM INSTRUCTIONS

Nearly anywhere you have a blank wall, you can design and install a wire shelving system that fits your specific storage and organization needs. For example, my laundry room originally had quite a bit of unused wall space. The room isn't large, but it does have some unused wall space I was keen on taking advantage of.

To begin, I installed short upright braces to three walls and then added the brackets to hold the wire shelves. Using the combination of braces and brackets enables me to adjust the height of my shelves as necessary.

I then installed a shelf close to the ceiling that wrapped around all three walls. The brand of wire shelving I used offered a hanging rod on the bottom of the shelf as well as hooks for extra storage.

On the wall facing the washer and dryer, where I had more vertical space to work with, I added more wire shelving, this time with longer uprights and more brackets with shorter shelves.

By evaluating where I wasn't using my walls effectively, and planning what combination of wire system products would help me maximize the space I had available, I was able to create an area for organization with lots of surplus storage. For more how-to information and inspirational photos, visit thecreativityexchange.com/organizing-your-life.

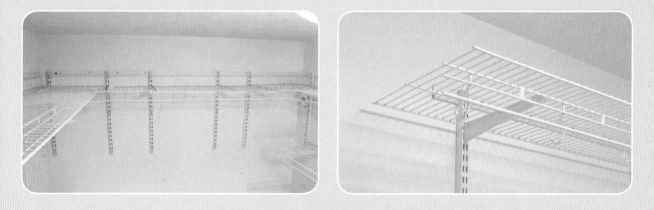

Before you get started with the installation, be sure to locate and mark the studs in your wall.

after

TRICK #1
INSTALL ROWS OF HOOKS

Adding a row of small hooks in a narrow area such as the laundry room is an easy way to use wasted space and create more storage options. Use these hooks to hang empty laundry bags, mesh washing bags, and cleaning supplies like brooms or feather duster. Multi-hook units you can install on the wall come in many different sizes and styles so you're sure to find something you can use.

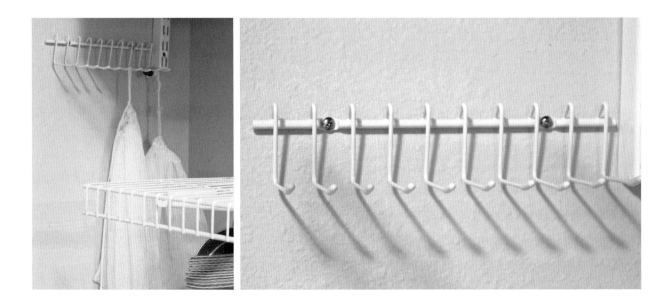

TRICK #2
ADD A SHELF NEXT TO THE WASHER

Floating shelves are easy to install and come in a variety of styles. Plus, they often don't take up a lot of space. If you're limited on shelf space in your laundry room, consider installing a a floating shelf next to your washing machine. This is the perfect spot to hold stain-remover pens, scissors, and the little stuff you need as you put clothes in the washer. Add clear glass candleholders or small jars to contain smaller items.

CHECKLIST

LAUNDRY ROOM

notes

storage pieces

 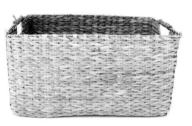

quick tricks

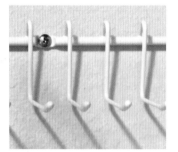 

inspiration

CLEANDESIGNPARTNERS.COM
DONNA DOTAN PHOTOGRAPHY
SANDANDSISAL.COM
THECREATIVITYEXCHANGE.COM

tips

- On the wall behind the laundry room door, hang wall storage pieces that can hold mops, brooms, dusters, and more.

- Opt for shelving or cabinets that fill the space all the way up to the ceiling. Keep a step ladder in the laundry room so you can access these upper areas easily.

- Adjust shelving to fit each storage piece to make the most of the space available.

- Make use of stackable plastic bins to organize lots of little stuff.

- Next to a laundry sink or behind the washer and dryer, install narrow shelving traditionally used in bathrooms to organize small things.

- Hang over-the-door baskets inside cabinet doors to provide additional storage.

- Assess your trouble spots. Take a close look at your laundry room on its worst day and pinpoint the areas and items that seem the most unorganized. For example, if clothes are frequently tossed on top of the washer and dryer waiting to be folded, consider incorporating tall expandable laundry hampers in cabinets (you might have to remove a shelf) or underneath shelving to store clean clothes until you have time to fold them.

- Use plastic storage bins, small wood crates, or baskets to help organize cabinets or shelves.

- Tuck old trays, caddies, and buckets in and around the laundry room and underneath sink areas to hold whatever stray items you need them to hold.

CLOSETS

Closets can be a challenging space to organize because they can quickly become a catch-all for stuff you don't know what to do with or have room for elsewhere. It can get so bad, you might dread even thinking about the idea of organizing a closet and feel overwhelmed when you door. But you can get control over your closets!

The key to getting and keeping your closets organized is to not empty out the closet all at once because it's too tempting to just give up later and put everything back without seeing your organizing attempt through to completion. If you work section by section, a little at a time, you eventually will get there—and won't be overwhelmed by seeing the closet contents scattered all over the room. If you choose the right storage pieces to maximize the space you have, you can sometimes double the amount of storage space in available in your closet.

1 GROUP CLOTHING

Hanging or grouping clothes by length creates additional storage underneath the shorter items.

2 SMALL HOOKS

Install a row of small wall hooks to store necklaces, bracelets, and other jewelry out in the open where you can see what you have.

3 STORAGE BASKETS

Store out-of-season clothes and shoes out of the way in baskets on the upper shelves of your closet. This gives you more room below for in-season items.

4 SHOE SHELVES

Install shelves or use premade shoe shelving units at the bottom of your closet—especially below your hanging clothes—to keep all your shoes in neat order.

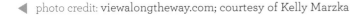

◀ photo credit: viewalongtheway.com; courtesy of Kelly Marzka

Master Closet Transformation

A newly updated and organized closet can quickly become your favorite room in your house. Don't be surprised to find yourself standing in the doorway, admiring how pretty it is and how everything is perfectly in its right place. Of course, you'll be able to find what you're looking for quicker and easier, too.

DIY PROJECT #9

MATERIALS

SHEETS OF MDF BOARD

SCREWS

PRIMER

PAINT

SHORT CLOSET ROD

SHOWER CURTAIN HOOKS

SHORT TOWEL BARS

SMALL HOOKS

BASKETS

TOOLS

PENCIL

TAPE MEASURE

STUD FINDER

SAW

DRILL

DRILL BITS

PAINTBRUSH

PAINTER'S TAPE

Is your closet a mess with shoes strewn all over the floor, clothes hung haphazardly, and shelves crammed with various and random items? You can transform it into an organized space—without the need for a professional organizer! Kelly Marzka of viewalongtheway.com transformed her relatively small and disheveled closet into a beautifully organized and functional space. She designed the shelving to specifically fit her space, constructed it out of sheets of MDF board, and painted it with a coat of primer and then paint.

after

In this vanity area, several small screws hold necklaces long and short on the sides, and a clear plastic mail organizer serves as a stand for clutch purses. Below, drawers (constructed from the same MDF) hold smaller pieces of jewelry like rings and earrings.

Under the vanity area, a short closet rod and some shower curtain hooks provide an out-of-the-way spot for handbag storage.

Most of the functional storage is on the left side. Here, Kelly has all out-of-season clothes in baskets, stored at the top of the closet, out of the way. In-season clothes hang below, over shelves that corral shoes.

In a narrow space next to the hanging clothes, she has a slide-out scarf organizer where scarfs are looped around short towel bars.

Shelves below offer orderly and compact shoe storage.

Kelly is thrilled with how her closet has been transformed with some clever storage solutions and some help from her handy husband, who built the custom pieces. For more details and additional images, go to viewalongtheway.com.

▲ photo credit: viewalongtheway.com; courtesy of Kelly Marzka

CREATIVE
STORAGE IDEAS

1 **DRESSERS**

Move dressers you're not using in other rooms into your closet. If they're short, tuck them under shorter hanging clothes. This frees up space in other rooms and gives you more closet storage. If you can, choose pieces that match to give your closet that "built-in" look.

2 **JEWELRY BOXES**

Oversize jewelry boxes or wood tool storage boxes are fantastic all-in-one storage pieces for jewelry. They hold a variety of accessories in a compact space and offer tiny compartments for small pieces like rings and earrings. Opt for a color that matches your other closet storage pieces if you can.

If you're going to put shelving on your top shelves, flip over the shelves as you assemble them so the colored sides face down, where you'll be able to see them as you stand in the closet below and look up.

Cloth storage bins are the perfect size to slip in wherever you have pockets of wasted space. Consider using them to toss belts, scarves or folded t-shirts.

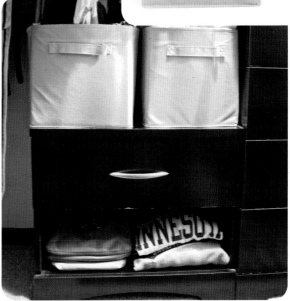

3   SHOE SHELVING UNITS

The number-one wasted space in closets is up at the ceiling. By adding premade shoe shelving units on your closet's top shelves, you create additional storage for shoes, out-of-season sweaters, or anything else you want to store up and out of the way.

4   SMALLER STORAGE PIECES

Look around your favorite department store, and you're sure to find some inexpensive nightstands or end tables (preferably with drawers). These shorter storage pieces are perfect for tucking in your closet where larger and taller items like a dresser won't fit.

CREATIVE
ACCESSORY ORGANIZING

1 **TRUNKS**
Decorative trunks are a great option for storing keepsakes or out-of-season clothing neatly and out of sight. Add them to upper shelves in your closet where they're out of the way.

2 **TRAYS**
Use shallow trays as catch-alls for loose jewelry and accessories. Or place them where you can use them for a quick and easy home for items you use every day, such as your watch or an employee security badge.

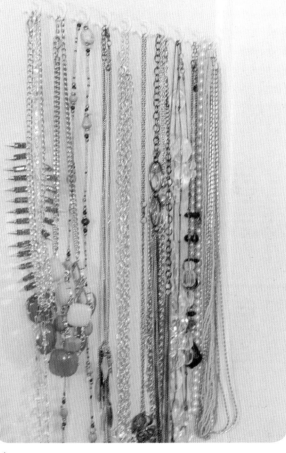

3 DRAWERS

If you have a dresser in your closet, consider using the top drawer for accessory storage. It's a great way to keep all the little stuff in check and hidden away but still very accessible. Be sure to add a drawer organizer or two!

4 HOOKS

Hooks can have countless uses and are an organizer's best friend. Available in nearly any size imaginable, hooks are ideal for holding necklaces, belts, scarves, and more in your closet. Install several in a row for a tidy display.

▲ photo credits: viewalongtheway.com; courtesy of Kelly Marzka

Printable Closet Organization Worksheet

Use this handy worksheet to finally get your unruly closet under control! (To use the printable, go to thecreativityexchange.com/organizing-your-life, download the worksheet file, and print on 8¹/₂×11-inch/21.5×28cm paper!)

1 USING A PENCIL (NOT A PEN), DRAW A ROUGH SKETCH OF THE INSIDE OF YOUR CLOSET:

2 RANK, IN ORDER, YOUR CLOSET'S TOP THREE PROBLEMS:

_____ not enough space for shoes

_____ not enough space for handbags

_____ not enough space for accessories

_____ not enough drawer space

_____ not enough hanging space

_____ not enough space to hang pants

_____ not enough space to hang long pieces

_____ too many clothes

_____ other _____

_____

_____

3 LOOK AT YOUR TOP THREE TROUBLE SPOTS, DETERMINE WHAT YOU NEED TO SOLVE THOSE PROBLEMS, AND RANK THEM IN ORDER:

_____ more hanging space

_____ more drawer space

_____ more storage space for shoes

_____ more storage space for handbags

_____ more storage space for folded items

_____ more storage space for accessories

_____ more space for clothes hamper

_____ more hanging space for _____

_____ more shelving for _____

_____ more specialized storage for _____

_____ other _____

_____

4 Determine what areas of your closet are wasted space or spots where you could create new organization opportunities. Circle these areas on your sketch. Then ask yourself:

- What areas am I currently not maximizing?
- Could I move any storage pieces currently in my closet to other areas if they work better somewhere else?
- What hanging pieces could I move around or add to maximize the space available?

5 Go back to your closet and measure the areas you circled on your sketch. Write these dimensions on your sketch.

6 Determine what color storage pieces will best coordinate with the trim and shelving in your closet. Note that if you choose any color other than white, dark brown, or black, you might have some difficulty finding standard storage pieces.

7 Search online for new storage pieces. Be sure to carefully check dimensions and look for color options that are close to your trim/shelving color. Also try to make the most of your space available by choosing storage pieces that are functional and won't leave you with any wasted space. Bookmark or list here the storage pieces you're interested in:

_____

_____

_____

_____

_____

_____

8 Draw the potential new storage pieces in your sketch of your closet, and erase and move any existing storage changes you can make. This helps you come to a decision on what storage pieces you should purchase.

9 Purge your closet of any unwanted items. A good rule of thumb is if you haven't worn it or used it for a year, get rid of it.

10 Instead of empting out your whole closet to begin your reorganization, work section by section, incorporating and filling new storage pieces as you go. This way you can step away from reorganizing for a day or two and not be tempted to just give up and put everything back where it was.

11 As you finish adding your new storage pieces, take note of areas where you could employ more baskets, bins, and other special smaller pieces to keep your closet organized—for good.

For more information, visit thecreativityexchange.com/organizing-your-life. And enjoy your new closet!

CHILDREN'S CLOSETS

1 COORDINATING COLORS

Organize your child's clothes by color so you can find what you're looking for easily. Use matching hangers to give the closet a unified look.

Baskets are always a great choice for storing small accessories.

2 SHOE SHELVING UNITS

Stack several premade shoe shelving units for easy storage of sweaters, accessories, and other commonly used items.

Plastic bins can be used to corral summer sandles and flip-flops.

3 FABRIC BINS

Inexpensive and readily available, fabric storage bins hold and hide seasonal clothes out of the way.

4 HANGING SHOE STORAGE UNITS

Install hanging shoe storage units on the back of closet doors to get shoes up off the floor. And these aren't just for shoes! Tuck scarves, hats, and earmuffs here as well for easy access.

1 **ORGANIZE LIKE ITEMS**
Organizing like items is important in a catch-all area. This way you can tell what you have at a glance rather than having to search for a certain piece.

2 **DRAWERS FOR LITTLE THINGS**
Small dressers in a closet can help keep the little things organized and less likely to become lost or tossed elsewhere.

Dedicate a hall or guest room closet as your "junk" closet to hold anything you can't find a suitable home for someplace else. Decorations, extra picture frames, craft supplies, surplus linens—this is the perfect spot to store these things. Plus, having one catch-all closet for all these items means you can find them quicker and easier and they're not strewn about the rest of your home, taking up space you could use for other things.

Catch-All Closet Cubbies

If your closet is on the verge of becoming an out-of-control mess of items you don't know where else to put anywhere else, this project is for you. Best of all, it's easy to implement and fairly inexpensive. With the help of some simple-to-assemble premade closet storage pieces, you can tuck every last item in your closet in its rightful, organized place.

MATERIALS

PREMADE CLOSET
STORAGE CUBES

PREMADE SHOE
SHELVING UNITS

TOOLS

TOOLS SPECIFIED BY STORAGE CUBE AND
SHOE SHELVING UNIT INSTRUCTIONS

The keys to this project, like so many others, are careful planning, a smart design, and making the most of the space available.

Start by looking at your closet. Really look at it. Where do you have unused space? Maybe, like I did, you have a wall with a shelf and a rod that's meant to hang clothes that you're not using for that purpose. Instead, stuff is just stacking up on the floor below the shelf in a chaotic mess. Why not fill that wall with storage cubbies to organize all your stuff? You could triple the amount of storage you have!

After I measured my wall space available, I purchased inexpensive premade closet storage cubes, brought them home, and put them together. Assembly only took about 20 minutes, and I was surprised how sturdy and well made they are for the price.

I bought a few units: I got a six-cube unit for the left side of the wall and a nine-cube unit for the right side. This filled my wall with cubes. I also purchased a few premade shoe shelving units and popped them on top of the cube units for additional storage up by the ceiling. I placed a second six-cube unit on its side at the bottom of my closet.

Then I filled the cubes with baskets and bins to house various types of items neatly and orderly. No more chaotic mess! For more how-to information and inspirational photos, visit thecreativityexchange.com/organizing-your-life.

before

after

CATCH-ALL CLOSET CUBBIES

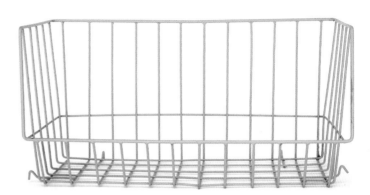

1 WIRE SHELVING

Wire shelving is a valuable addition to any closet. These shelving units are inexpensive and usually very easy to install.

2 WIRE BINS

Use large wire bins to keep washcloths and hand towels in order and easy to find.

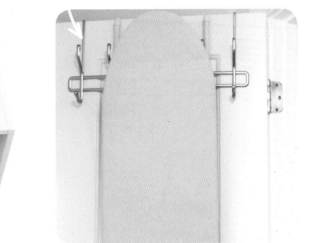

3 SHOE SHELVING UNITS

Premade shoe shelving units hold more than just shoes! Add these versatile storage solutions to shelves to give yourself additional surfaces to hold sheets, towels, and more.

4 OVER-THE-DOOR STORAGE

Don't overlook the space on the back of your closet door. Hang specialized hook units here, such as multi-hook units or those designed to hold irons and ironing boards.

THE
CRAFT CLOSET

1 **PEGBOARD**
Pegboard is a fantastic way to organize and store supplies with hooks, baskets, and other storage attachments.

2 **PEGBOARD HOOKS**
You can store just about anything on pegboard hooks beyond what they were designed to hold. Think creatively and use different size hooks to hold scissors, tools, buckets, and even rods to house rolls of ribbon and twine.

3 **BRACKETS AND SHELVES**
Install shelving with brackets (secured to the studs for extra strength) in the top of your closet. Use this shelving to hold books, baskets, craft supplies, and other heavier items safely.

4 **LARGE BASKETS**
Large, bin-style baskets serve as easy catch-alls for holding miscellaneous items. You can easily pull out the basket to find what you need and then tuck it back away to avoid lots of clutter.

 photo credit: beneathmyheart.net; courtesy of Traci Hutcherson

TRICK #1
SPRAY PAINT MISMATCHED CRATES AND OTHER STORAGE PIECES

You don't have to go out and buy all new matching storage pieces to get organized. You can use what you likely already have around your house and give the mismatched pieces a unified look with spray paint. If your items are plastic, be sure you use primer and paint specifically designed for use with plastic. Follow the manufacturers' instructions for prep and top coat of your various plastic crates, beverage carriers, or other plastic pieces. Let them dry completely before filling them and tucking them into your closet.

TRICK #2
CREATIVE BAG STORAGE

If you have several different-size bags taking up space in various areas of your closets, try this quick trick: instead of storing several bags separately, group them together in a large, narrow, sturdy plastic tote bag with handles. Fold all your totes and bags flat, and tuck them into the large plastic tote. Pull out all the handles so you can remove the bag you want without disturbing the rest of the bags.

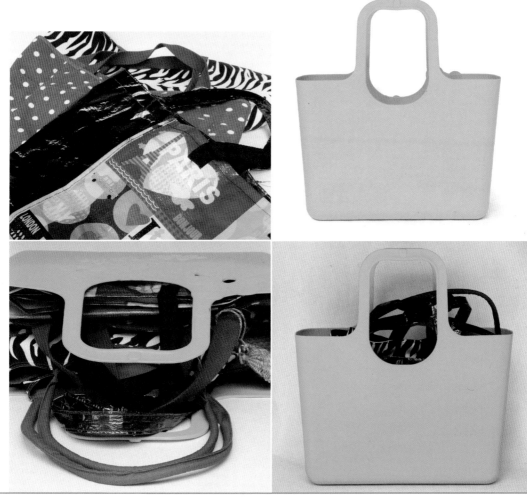

CHECKLIST

CLOSETS

notes

storage pieces

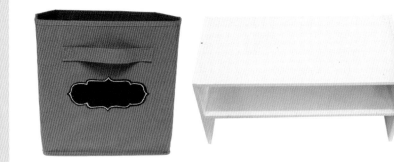

quick tricks

inspiration

BENEATHMYHEART.NET
THECREATIVITYEXCHANGE.COM
VIEWALONGTHEWAY.COM

tips

- Look up! The top of the closet is a great source of additional storage. If you have open shelving at the top of your closet, add shoe shelving all the way around to provide an additional shelf for shoes—or anything else.

- Maximize the space below hanging clothes. Slide a short, two-door dresser underneath shirts, and you instantly create extra storage.

- Fill a closet wall with narrow cube storage units. The individual cube compartments can help keep things separated and in order.

- Make the most of shelf space with plastic stackable bins. They're ideal for organizing small items.

- Add a narrow dresser to a clothes closet, junk closet, or craft closet, and fill the drawers with deep drawer organizing pieces to corral all kinds of things.

- Use over-the-door, multitiered wire basket storage pieces to provide additional storage for accessories and smaller items.

- Assess your trouble spots. Look at your closet floor when it's unorganized. What types of items do you see there? If your problem is shoes or handbags, consider incorporating additional shoe storage on a shelf or try over-the-door shoe and handbag holders. What other items always seem to be disorganized? Look for specific organization pieces to store these items, whatever they might be.

- If you don't have room for a dresser, see if an end table with shelving will fit in your closet to incorporate more storage.

- Use crates, baskets, and bins to catch sandals, flip-flops, and tennis shoes in clothes closets, supplies in craft closets, and miscellaneous little stuff in junk closets.

BEDROOMS

The bedroom is one of the most underutilized rooms in the home when it comes to organizing and incorporating storage. The reason for this is often because we want to keep this restful place, where we relax and recharge, as free of clutter as possible. And that's understandable. But the truth is, by incorporating just a few storage pieces in your bedroom, you can free up space in your closets or elsewhere without adding clutter to your restful room.

So many fantastic hidden-storage pieces are available today, and many are ideal for the bedroom. Using these pieces to store out-of-season clothing, shoes, or items that seem to always be overflowing elsewhere can make a huge impact. The key to bedroom organization is choosing furniture pieces with the maximum amount of storage and functionality and thinking about creative ways you can take advantage of this underutilized space.

◄ photo credit: Amanda Carol Interiors

1 **FUNCTIONAL NIGHTSTANDS**
Choosing the right nightstand can make all the difference when organizing your bedroom. Rather than simple tables, choose nightstands that offer additional storage in drawers and shelves.

2 **UNDER THE BED**
With the right boxes, baskets, bins, or trays, you can transform the space under your bed—an area that's often overlooked and forgotten about as an organizing opportunity—into a beneficial storage spot.

3 **BASKETS**
If you're like me, reading material close to the bed is a must. Add baskets or other storage pieces to your nightstand or next to your bed to hold reading materials.

4 **ARMOIRES**
Armoires have many uses in the bedroom beyond just storing clothes. Use the bottom part to store clothes but then set your TV in the top so you can close it away when you're not using it. Add baskets or decorative trunks to the very top for even more storage.

1 BENCHES

A guest room bench offers extra seating and a spot for your visitors to set their suitcases.

2 DECORATIVE BOXES

Provide small decorative boxes around the room your guest can use for his or her jewelry, watch, wallet, etc. This helps keep those items secure and less likely to get lost.

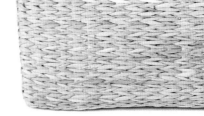

3 NESTING TABLES

Nesting tables allow for extra storage and tabletop surfaces when you want them but then easily tuck, or nest, back together when not in use. They're very versatile and handy for guests to pull out and use around the room as they like.

◀ photo credit: Jenna Buck Gross

4 LARGER BASKETS

Set a larger basket in the guest room in which your guests can drop their used towels and linens. This keeps them off the floor or another piece of furniture (especially wet towels) and makes it easier for you to find and grab when you're ready to do laundry.

THE
NIGHTSTAND

1 LIDDED BOXES

Add a lidded box to your nightstand to hold pens and paper, headphones or phone charge cords, and other items you might need while you're in bed. This keeps these items within reach but closes away the clutter, out of sight.

2 PLANTERS

A small decorative garden planter is a pretty and functional way to contain remotes, cell phones, pens, and other nightstand necessities.

3 NIGHTSTAND SHELVES

If your nightstand has a bottom shelf, it can be home to a basket or bin in which you keep books and magazines, cords and accessories for your phone or tablet, flashlights, or other items you want close to your bed.

4 NIGHTSTAND DRAWERS

When possible, opt for a nightstand that has one or more drawers for additional storage. If you charge your phone or tablet on your nightstand, you can convert a drawer into a hidden charging station by drilling a hole in the back of the drawer through which to run cords.

CREATIVE
STORAGE IDEAS

1 **NIGHTSTAND WITH DRAWERS AND CLOSED-DOOR STORAGE**
Choosing a nightstand with lots of additional storage in drawers and hidden storage can help keep the bedroom organized. A narrow dresser is a smart alternative to a traditional nightstand.

2 **STORAGE BENCHES**
A storage bench or large ottoman at the end of the bed can serve as extra seating as well as provide additional organizing opportunities. Tuck out-of-season clothes, extra blankets, or other items commonly stored in the closet here instead to free up space in the closet.

▲ photo credit: Kirkland's

▲ photo credit: Kirkland's

3 ARMOIRES

Tall armoires or wardrobes are ideal in the bedroom because these pieces maximize space from the floor to the ceiling. Look for an armoire constructed with drawers in the bottom half for clothes or blankets and an upper area with doors behind which you can set a television.

4 DRESSERS

Larger dressers and chests of drawers offer as an upper surface upon which you can organize books, jewelry, or other accessories as well as hidden storage below. The more drawers the dresser has, the more you can separate and organize folded items.

▲ photo credit: Amanda Carol Interiors

1 **CORNER BOOKSHELVES**
Corner bookshelves fill that space in the corner of a child's bedroom where nothing else seems to fit. Fill the shelves with baskets and bins for easy-access storage.

2 **NIGHTSTANDS**
A functional nightstand with lots of storage is essential in a child's room. Use the drawer to contain small items; the open storage below is perfect for bedtime books.

3 **UNDER-THE-BED OPTIONS**
The space under the bed usually goes unused, not only in children's bedrooms, but in adult and guest bedrooms, too. Make the most of this area with a few shallow storage boxes used to hold keepsakes, out-of-season clothes, or extra shoes.

4 **CABINETS AND SHELVES**
Bookshelves and other cabinets are handy throughout the house, but they're especially useful in children's rooms. Set them up to house frequently used toys, books, and other items, and encourage your children to return their things to the shelves when they're done with them.

1 OPEN SHELVES

Open shelves provide space for games, books, toys, etc. in sight and within easy reach.

Rethink where you can use kitchen storage pieces, like these candy jars.

2 CANDY JARS

Clear, lidded jars are a great way to help kids organize smaller items. The lids keep everything in place and reduce the chances of spills. Group several on a shelf for a unified look.

3 TRUNKS

Trunks of any size are useful in children's rooms. They provide hidden storage for just about anything.

4 PLASTIC TUBS

Recycle large plastic food tubs as fun and functional see-through storage pieces.

CREATIVE STORAGE

1 REUSE PACKAGING
Don't throw away the boxes your child's toys come in. Instead, use them to store the item when not in use. Your child will recognize the packaging and immediately know that's where the toy belongs.

2 MAGAZINE HOLDERS
Paper is essential in many childhood crafts and projects. Instead of having a lot of loose paper laying around, turn magazine holders on their sides and use to store craft paper, notebooks, magazines, etc.

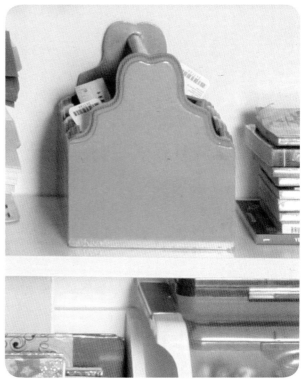

3 **EASY-ACCESS BINS AND BASKETS**
It can be difficult to get children to clean up after themselves. Make it easier for them by having bins and baskets housed on lower shelves at their eye level and easy to reach. Encourage your children to keep their space tidy by tossing their toys, books, and other play items in these bins for quick cleanup.

4 **SMALL CADDIES WITH HANDLES**
A small caddy with handles allows children to carry craft supplies or toys from one place to another with very little effort.

DESK

Colorful baskets with dividers can store almost anything!

1 **TOOL BOXES**
Look for storage solutions that work for you. For example, a tool box isn't just for holding tools in the garage. It can be brought into the house and used to organize all sorts of supplies.

2 **WALL POCKETS**
Adhere bins, baskets, and wall pockets above your child's desk to hold paper, pens, and other craft supplies, reducing desktop clutter.

3 **STORAGE BOXES**
Coordinating cardboard or plastic boxes designed to hold magazines, photos, or shoes can house pictures, projects, and other items up and out of the way. Be sure to label the boxes so you know at a glance what's in them!

4 **DESK ORGANIZERS**
Rather than taking up space on the desk with two separate single-use items, choose dual-purpose products such as this combination lamp/desk organizer.

TOY BOX

Inside

Bench–style toy boxes (or large storage ottomans) help keep children's spaces organized, provide hidden storage, and offer extra seating. Slide handled totes, bags, or plastic containers into the toy box and use them to group toys by activity. During playtime, your child can pull out just the tote containing the toys he or she wants to play with and leave everything else neatly inside the box. When playtime is over, cleanup is quick and easy. Just toss the toys back into the tote and slide the tote back in it's spot in the toy box.

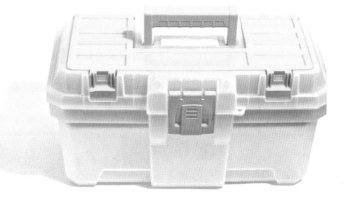

1   **PLASTIC CARRY TOTES**
Use inexpensive plastic totes with handles to house dolls, dress-up accessories, stuffed animals, etc. toys together by activity. Your little one can then pull out just the tote he or she wants to play with.

2   **TOOL BOXES**
Tool boxes are a great option for storing small toys, crafts, or other activities together in one grab-and-go container.

Toy Box Re-Cover

I enjoy repurposing furniture when I can to give new life to something I'm no longer using for its original purpose—and make it a pretty piece in which to organize! Here, I show you how to revamp an old toy box bench into a hip new storage ottoman.

MATERIALS

TOY BOX BENCH

WHITE TWILL FABRIC

UPHOLSTERY NAIL TACKS

DECORATIVE GIMP TRIM

BRASS NAIL HEADS

4-INCH (10CM) POLY FOAM CUSHIONS

BATTING

UPHOLSTERY FABRIC

TOOLS

HAMMER

SCISSORS

PENCIL

BREAD KNIFE

HOT GLUE GUN

HOT GLUE

STAPLE GUN

SCREWDRIVER

First I removed the old fabric-covered lid and the decorative nail heads holding on the fabric.

Using 4 yards (3.75m) of white twill fabric, and allowing for a hem at the bottom and excess fabric to go over the lip separating the lid and the storage part of the bench, I tacked on the first wraparound layer of fabric using upholstery nail tacks placed on the inside of the bench. I stared wrapping on the far left side and ended on the back by folding in and tacking the fabric.

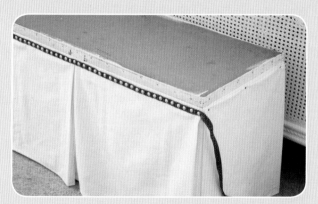

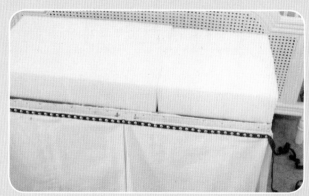

I measured and marked where the faux panels would go. To that measure, I added 1 inch (2.5cm) on both sides so I could fold in and hem the sides. I then measured from the floor to where I'd nail the top of the panel to the front of the bench and added $3/4$ inch (2cm) to fold the top over and nail. I attached the faux panels using upholstery nails.

I covered the top edges of the faux panels with decorative gimp trim and secured it with brass nail heads about every $1^1/_2$ inches (3.75cm).

I then cut two 4-inch (10cm) poly foam cushions to fit the top of the bench and hot glued the foam pieces to each other and to the bench. I covered the foam with a layer of batting, stretched smooth and tight, and nailed it to the lid.

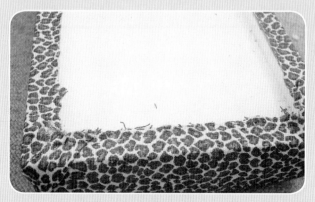

after

I then covered the cushion with upholstery fabric stapled it in place. Finally, I reattached the back hinges to the lid and to the bottom part of the bench.

By reusing a piece I already had, I was able to save money and get a fun and functional "new" storage piece! For more how-to information and photos, visit thecreativityexchange.com/organizing-your-life.

CHILDREN'S CREATIVE
STORAGE IDEAS

1 MAIL ORGANIZERS

Move bill and letter organizers from the office into your child's room to store party invitations, birthday cards, pen pal letters, or school projects neatly on his or her desk.

2   **LARGE PLASTIC TOTES**
Not only do these decorative carriers
add a pop of color to your child's room;
they also provide extra storage that's
easy to pick up and carry around.

3   **COORDINATING BASKETS**
Spray paint mismatched baskets or bins
in colors that match your child's room.
This gives old items new life and provides a home for books and magazines.

TRICK #1
REPURPOSE LARGE PLASTIC SNACK CONTAINERS

Don't toss out those bulk-size plastic food tubs you get at warehouse and wholesale stores. Instead, wash the lid and container by hand when it's empty (not in the dishwasher, where it could melt), remove the label, and use in your child's room to hold balls, small toys, and other little items. Place the tub on a shelf or cabinet your little one can reach for easy access. Be sure to keep the lid to avoid accidental spills!

TRICK #2
USE SWIVEL-STYLE POWER STRIPS

A quick trick for keeping cords and and plugs organized in tight spots such as behind beds and nightstands is to use swivel-style power strips that twist to the side so plugs are parallel to the wall instead of perpendicular to it. This makes it easier to access and use the plugs and also allows you to push furniture closer to the wall. You can label each cord by writing on a piece of tape and folding the tape over the cord for quick identification.

CHECKLIST BEDROOMS

notes

_____

_____

_____

_____

_____

_____

_____

_____

_____

_____

_____

_____

_____

_____

_____

_____

_____

_____

_____

_____

storage pieces

quick tricks

inspiration

AMANDACAROLINTERIORS.COM

COLORDRUNK.BLOGSPOT.COM

KIRKLAND'S

THECREATIVITYEXCHANGE.COM

tips

- Take advantage of an unused wall to hold an additional dresser, armoire, or wardrobe to create more organizing and storage opportunities.

- Set an upholstered storage bench at the end of your bed, and use it to store sweaters, blankets, or bedroom linens. As a bonus, it doubles as extra seating.

- Employ large baskets in corners or next to nightstands or dressers as catch-alls for books, magazines, and other items.

- Add a small table next to a bedroom chair for an additional tabletop that can hold decorative bowls or wooden boxes for neatly storing smaller items.

- Fill the tops of armoires, bedroom media centers, and wardrobes with pretty baskets to organize rarely used items.

- Assess your trouble spots. Look around your room and determine what items seem to continually clutter your bedroom. Pinpointing those things you regularly have to pick up helps you think about what solutions you need to help better organize your space. For example, if clothing and shoes are a problem, that may be a sign that you need to create more storage in your closet and dressers. Having a very large decorative basket in the bedroom is a great spot in which you can quickly toss items to organize later but still keep the bedroom clutter-free.

- Set a narrow bookshelf along an unused wall, and fill it with coordinating baskets to house a variety of items.

- Arrange small decorative garden urns, glass trays, or pretty wood boxes on nightstands and dresser tops to store little things.

NURSERY

If you have a baby, you also have a lot of the stuff that comes along with having a little one. Diapers, clothes, toys, baby care and transportation items—the nursery is home to so many little things that without good storage solutions, this room can get out of control quickly.

Key to organizing a nursery is focusing on the function of the room and choosing storage pieces that work for the way you use the space. Setting up a nursery based on tasks and grouping together everything related to that task in open shelving helps save time and extra steps. Organize all diaper-related items together, all sleep-related things together, and all play-related pieces together.

◄ photo credit: Molly Scott

1 **DRAWERS**
Organizing inside the drawers is important for any room but more so in the nursery. Storing like items together helps minimize the time you spend changing and dressing your little one by keeping everything neatly within your reach.

2 **CHANGING TABLE DIAPER STATION**
When you're changing your baby, you want all the products and supplies you need close by so you don't have to walk around to get anything. Use a bin or try to hold these items.

3 **BOOKSHELVES**
When placing a bookshelf in a nursery, set it horizontal, like a bench, rather than vertical. This helps create a safe environment for your baby by keeping everything low to the ground and adds extra storage.

◄ photo credit: Molly Scott

4 **CRIB STORAGE**
A crib with a drawer underneath provides a handy place to store extra clothes, blankets, diapers, and other baby-related items.

CREATIVE
STORAGE IDEAS

1 CLOTH BINS

Inexpensive cloth storage bins come in countless patterns and colors and are a smart solution for organizing changing tables.

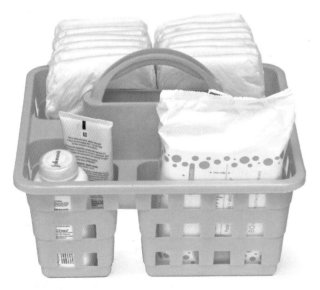

2 CADDIES

Stock a plastic caddy with diapers, wipes, and other changing supplies for a grab-and-go diaper-changing tote.

3 **WIRE CART**

Turn a wire cart into a mobile baby care unit you can move around the house as needed. Keeping the cart full of blankets, toys, books, and diaper-changing supplies where you need it means you don't have to run back and forth to the nursery as often.

4 **CUBBIES**

Cube storage units are ideal in the nursery because the compartments are the perfect size to hold all the little stuff that comes with a baby. Use a unit in the closet to store baby shoes, socks, and clothes, or secure the unit to a wall next to the changing table and fill with diapers, powder, and lotions for quick and easy access. Or connect two units together and secure to the wall for even more small-cube storage.

TRICK #1
PRINTABLE NURSERY LABELS

The nursery is often a very colorful room, and you can add even more color with these fun printable labels. To use these labels, go to thecreativityexchange.com/organizing-your-life, and download the blank label template. Either print the blank labels on 8½×11-inch (21.5×28cm) label paper and write on them with a marker or chalk pen, or fill in the labels on your computer using image-editing software and then print. Adhere the labels to your buckets.

TRICK #2
INSTALL FLOATING BOOK-SHELVES

Cluster several floating shelves together on a nursery wall for a unique twist on bookshelves. This adds a pop of fun and color to a nursery wall and also provides easy access to baby's favorite books when it's story time. For safety, be sure to use shelves that have a ridge, or edge, to keep the books in place, and use toggle bolts when attaching them to the wall for extra security as your baby grows and becomes mobile.

photo credit: Molly Scott ▶

CHECKLIST NURSERY

notes

storage pieces

quick tricks

inspiration

MOLLY SCOTT
THECREATIVITYEXCHANGE.COM

tips

- Utilize the space below the crib with under-the-crib storage pieces. This is a great place to store play toys that can be pulled out during play time. Add a crib bedskirt to hide the storage.

- Install open, floor-to-ceiling shelving pieces—bolted to the wall for safety—to maximize wall space and create additional storage.

- Add premade shoe storage units to the top shelves in the nursery closet for extra organizing opportunities.

- Opt for bin-style baskets. Most of the time you only have one free arm while you're in this room, holding your baby in your other arm.

- Use large, open, soft baskets in the nursery. They're safe for little ones and also are handy to corral items you can organize later.

- Consider long bread baskets for storing little stuff on shelves or in closets. They maximize the depth of a shelf.

- Assess your trouble spots. Look at the way your nursery is laid out and ask yourself what tasks seem the most challenging. For example, if you find yourself taking extra steps with the baby from the changing table to the closet, consider adding a row of baskets underneath the changing table for quick changes of clothing.

- Transform an old media or entertainment center to pretty open shelving by adding a shelf across the opening where the television would go and insert large baskets. Update the piece with a fresh coat of paint in fun, bright color. Bolt the unit to the wall for safety if you like.

- Load up a multitiered end table or a side table with open shelving with baskets for additional storage next to the rocker or along a blank wall.

PLAYROOM

Believe it or not, creating a space somewhere in your home for a playroom for your children goes a long way in getting *other* areas of your home organized. Converting a rarely used guest room, basement, family room—or even a large closet if you don't have another free room—into a dedicated play area helps keep toys, activities, and all the related little stuff corralled in one space and not strewn around your home.

Getting organized in the playroom means incorporating as many storage furniture pieces as possible, with deep bins and baskets for quick and easy cleanup. If your kids know where everything goes and it's easy for them to help tidy up their area, they're more likely to help keep things orderly. As a bonus, this is a wonderful opportunity to begin teaching them about organization and how to clean up after themselves!

◄ photo credit: iHeart Organizing

1 **MEDIA CENTER**
Using a bookshelf or entertainment center to create a kid's media center in the playroom is a great way to add additional storage for the television, games, toys, and craft supplies.

2 **DUAL-PURPOSE PIECES**
Maximize your space by using dual-purpose pieces. For instance, look for seating that also offers storage underneath. Or tip a sturdy bookshelf on its side and use it horizontally. Add a comfy cushion on top and baskets or bins below for storage.

3 **WALL POCKETS**
Playrooms can become disorganized very quickly. Keep more items up off the floor using wall pockets. You can buy specific wall storage pieces or mount crates or strong baskets to the wall. Keep them at your children's eye level so they can grab the books, toys, or games they want in a hurry.

4 **OPEN BASKETS/BINS**
Open baskets are important in a child's area. They enable easy access and make cleanup simple. Encourage your little ones to toss their toys in the appropriate bins when play time is over.

◀ photo credit: iHeart Organizing

TOY AND GAME
CONTAINMENT

1 **STORAGE CUBBIES**

Use storage cubes set low to the ground on your child's level to organize toys. Fill the cubes with plastic bins and baskets, and label them so your little one knows what goes where.

A low table is perfect for use in the playroom. Slip small storage ottomans underneath for both seating and another spot to hold toys and games.

2 **PLASTIC SHELVING UNITS**

Plastic shelving units in which you can slide drawers or tubs are a smart way to separate and organize toys and games.

3 **HANDLES, HANDLES, AND MORE HANDLES**
Opt for handles whenever you can in playroom storage. Handled caddies, bins, and buckets are perfect for storing little stuff, and your little ones can easily grab what they want and go.

4 **FABRIC BINS**
Lightweight fabric bins with handles are durable and light enough for children to easily pull out to access. These bins can hold and organize many items.

▲ photo credits: iHeart Organizing

1 DURABLE CONTAINERS

Use fabric bins, buckets, and caddies throughout the playroom to store almost anything, from movies and music to craft supplies and coloring books. The more durable and lightweight the containers are, the better for your little ones.

2 ADJUSTABLE SHELVES

If your media center or bookshelves have adjustable shelving, get creative with how you position the shelves. Adjust or remove shelves as necessary to store larger or taller toys.

Note: For safety, it's essential that you bolt or otherwise secure bookshelves and media centers to the wall in areas where your children will be.

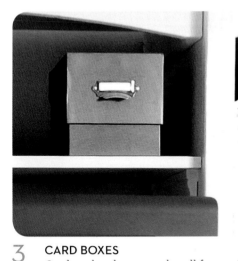

3 CARD BOXES

Card or shoe boxes work well for storing and organizing video games or DVDs.

4 UPPER SHELVES

You want to keep most of your children's toys, games, and activities where they're easy for the little ones to reach, but when it comes to expensive game systems, opt for the upper shelves. Keep them on the high shelves, where younger children can't reach them, to reduce the changes of these pricey systems getting broken or damaged.

◀ photo credits: iHeart Organizing

TRICK #1
CREATE AN ART BUCKET

Store kids' markers, crayons, and other craft supplies in a large bucket fitted with an organizer made to hold tools. (You can find these at your local home improvement store.) Slide the tool organizer over the bucket, fill with craft supplies, and set it next to or under the playroom table or somewhere your children can easily reach it. All your craft supplies have a home, and your children can carry it wherever they want to get creative.

TRICK #2
INSTALL FLOATING SHELVES

Create easy and nearly instant storage in the playroom using floating shelves. Securely attach them to the wall over shorter pieces of furniture to fill up that wasted the wall space. Fill the shelves with games, books, and other playroom items.

photo credit: iHeart Organizing ▶

CHECKLIST

PLAYROOM

notes

storage pieces

quick tricks

inspiration

iHEARTORGANIZING.BLOGSPOT.COM

THECREATIVITYEXCHANGE.COM

tips

- Choose shelving and furniture storage pieces that go from floor to ceiling—and bolt them to the wall for safety—to maximize wall space.

- Set a low toddler play table in the middle of the room, and tuck additional storage underneath.

- Install cube or cubby storage along unused walls to make the most of your space. Include separate areas for organizing toys and activities.

- Stock up on deep storage bins with wheels. Kids can push the bin to their play area and then it's right next to them when it's time for cleanup.

- Slide round plastic tubs with handles into cabinets to help contain the little stuff. Keep them on lower shelves so they're still accessible to little ones.

- Use large trays for ongoing activities like puzzles or crafts. They're easy to transfer to a shelf or cabinet for quick cleanup and pull out again later to continue the activity.

- Assess your trouble spots. Look at your playroom after you've tidied it up, and pinpoint what items are overflowing or don't have a good home. For example, if large toys seem to still be scattered and don't have a clear storage space, consider inexpensive, multitiered kitchen storage carts with wheels in the playroom closet or in a corner for storing these larger toys.

- Make liberal use of storage bins, baskets, or crates in the playroom. For a quick update, spray paint all these pieces in fun bright colors.

- Wash large, clear, pretzel or snack tubs when they're empty, and use them for see-through storage for small items.

OFFICE

It doesn't matter whether you have a dedicated room for an office or a desk tucked away in the corner of another room in your home; the steps for getting and keeping your office organized are the same. Choosing the right storage pieces to maximize your available area and organizing your office by task helps you improve your efficiency and order in your office.

Take an honest look around your office space, and identify those items or areas that aren't organized or could use more efficient storage pieces. At the same time, think about how you could better utilize and arrange your space. Taking the time to assess and identify your office trouble spots and creating long-term solutions can transform your office almost instantly.

1 DESK WITH STORAGE

It's importance to start with a desk with plenty of storage and drawer space. Your desk needn't be big and bulky either.

2 CABINETS OR SHELVES

Think about adding a simple cabinet or shelving unit above your workstation. This provides additional storage for books, supplies, and even a printer.

3 LARGE BASKETS/BINS

You can't go wrong by adding baskets or bins to your office space. These are ideal for tossing items into that you can sort or file away later. These handy containers enable you to keep your office clutter free and allow for quick cleanup.

4 BULLETIN BOARDS

Every office needs a bulletin board. Add a board (or two) in your office to pin reminders, to-do lists, photos, invitations, and other essential information you need to remember.

1 **DRAWERS**
Choose a desk with drawers (and overhead storage, too, if you can) so you have a proper place for all the papers, bills, notes, and other items that accumulate in the office.

2 **WALL POCKET ORGANIZERS**
Attach wall pocket organizers to doors and walls around your office. They keep important files and other paperwork easily accessible to your work area yet off your desk.

3 **DESK ORGANIZERS**
Your desktop is no place for clutter. Use multipurpose desk organizers to store frequently used items close by while keeping your desktop clear and usable.

4 **BULLETIN BOARDS**
Hang a bulletin board close to your desk, and use it to help you keep your desktop clutter free.

Converting a Desk to a Built-In

Custom-made built-ins are very nice, but they're also very expensive. Luckily, you can re-create the look of a built-in by using regular pieces of furniture, transforming them to more resemble their higher-priced counterparts. And you don't have to be a professional contractor to do it!

MATERIALS

DESK OR OTHER PIECE OF FURNITURE TO CONVERT

SANDPAPER

PRIMER

PAINT

DRAWER HARDWARE

TOOLS

PAINTBRUSH

SCREWDRIVER

I bought this desk from a friend who no longer needed it. It's a nice piece, made of solid wood, and it's in good condition. I really liked the idea of having everything I need for my office—the file cabinets, bulletin boards, the desk itself, and the paper sorter and cubbies up top—in one piece of furniture, but neither the color or the style is exactly what I wanted in my office/craft room.

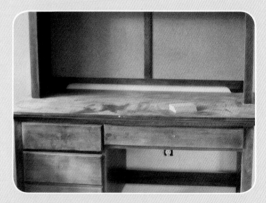

A coat of paint would fix the color. First I removed the knob pulls and sanded the entire piece.

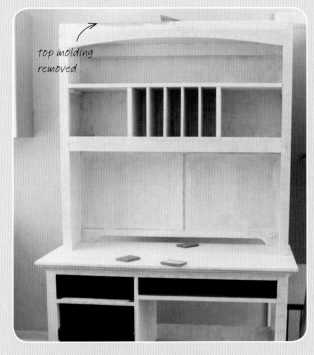

top molding removed

After removing the top molding to better fit the style I wanted, I added a coat of primer.

Then I painted the piece to coordinate with the colors in my office/craft room. (Note I didn't paint the area behind the bulletin board because it would be covered later when I updated the bulletin board.)

after

Finally, I added new hardware to the drawers and re-vamped the bulletin board.

I'm quite pleased with the finished piece. I've found it's the perfect piece of furniture to fit the space, and it really helps keep my office area organized! For more how-to information and inspirational photos, visit thecreativityexchange.com/organizing-your-life.

DESK ARMOIRE

1 **GET CREATIVE**
Paint or add wallpaper to the inside of an armoire to create a colorful, happy, and most importantly, defined workspace.

2 **DOOR ORGANIZERS**
Fit in organizing opportunities wherever you can. For example, paint the inside of the armoire doors with chalkboard paint or add corkboard (covered with fabric if you like) to hold to-do lists, notes, reminders, etc.

3 **MAXIMIZE SPACE**
Dedicate the bottom portion of the armoire as home your computer's hard drive, your printer, and trays for notebooks and important paperwork. You'll probably need to cut a small hole in the back of the armoire through which to run the power cords.

4 **SMALL ITEM ORGANIZERS**
Screw a metal plate to the inside of the armoire, and use magnetic tins and hooks to store paperclips, pins, staples, and other office-related items.

◀ photo credit: centsationalgirl.com; courtesy of Kate Riley

DESKTOP SOLUTIONS

1 GARDEN URNS

Garden urns and planters are an elegant way to store notebooks, files, cards, etc.

2 CLEAR PLASTIC CONTAINERS

Using clear plastic containers lets you see exactly what you have. Use these containers to store business cards, stamps, and receipts you want to hang on to.

3 MULTIPURPOSE DESK ORGANIZERS

Use narrow plastic storage organizers in and around your desk to corral commonly used items so you don't waste time searching for them. These small containers take up very little valuable desktop space and keep what you need handy.

4 MAIL ORGANZERS

Mail organizers are superb for keeping bills and mail neat and organized. Myriad sizes and styles are available so you're sure to find one that works in your space.

BULLETIN BOARD

1 CALENDARS AND CLIPBOARDS

Keep a calendar pinned to your bulletin board so you can remember important dates. A small clipboard is convenient for holding notes and lists on your bulletin board in a one grab-and-go group.

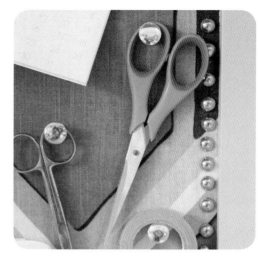

2 EXTRA-LARGE TACKS

Use extra-large thumbtacks to pin those office supplies you use most often like scissors or tape at your fingertips and ready for use.

3 SMALL CONTAINERS

Attach small containers to your bulletin board to keep little things from getting lost.

4 TO-DO LISTS

Pin your to-do list front and center on your bulletin board for quick reminders and easy access.

Bulletin Board Revamp

Organizing is about creating order out of chaos, and that applies to more than just the stuff in your closets, pantry, and garage. It also applies to your office, and especially your desk. A bulletin board can be an ideal way to organize your thoughts, to-do lists, bills, shopping lists, and so much more. If you have a blah and boring bulletin board, why not revamp it into something pretty you'll love to use?

MATERIALS

BULLETIN BOARD
FABRIC
THUMBTACKS OR
NAIL HEAD TACKS

TOOLS

PAINT SCRAPER OR BUTTER KNIFE
SCREWDRIVER
SCISSORS

My desk has built-in bulletin boards, but they were plain cork board—not very pretty, and not anything that inspired me to use them to organize my desk. A fun and chic fabric covering seemed quite appropriate!

Covering a bulletin board is an easy way to incorporate a pop of color and design into a space. And it doesn't take much fabric at all, so you can splurge on something really special if you like.

I removed the desk's back panel that holds the boards in place, centered and covered the boards with fabric, and inserted tacks in all four corners to secure the fabric. I returned the boards to the desk, and reattached the back panel. (If you're covering a free-standing framed bulletin board, center and cut your fabric to fit the inside of the frame, adding an extra 1 inch; 2.5cm of fabric on all four sides to tuck under the edge of the frame.)

DO IT YOURSELF

DIY PROJECT #14

I used a paint scraper (you also can use a butter knife) to tuck the fabric behind the desk frame and get it smooth and tight.

For a decorative touch, and to help keep the fabric in place, I added a nail head trim using standard office thumbtacks. I stuck tacks in all four corners first. Then, to ensure I added them evenly spaced around the edges, I stuck tacks in the midpoints of the boards. To finish, I continued adding tacks evenly around the edges.

after

I love the end result, and I use my pretty new bulletin boards so much! For more how-to information and inspirational photos, visit thecreativityexchange.com/organizing-your-life.

OFFICE DRAWERS

1 DRAWER ORGANIZERS

Expandable silverware drawer organizers are designed to hold more and, therefore, maximize more drawer space, than traditional office drawer organizers. A quick coat of spray paint can liven up the color.

2 BAKING CUPS

Sturdy paper baking cups make inexpensive storage for small items. They're fun and colorful and easy to move around to fit the space available.

3 NOTE CARD STORAGE

Silverware organizers, especially the expandable versions, often have a large spot in the back that's ideal for holding stationery, note cards, and other slightly larger items.

4 TRAYS

Small decorative trays are a great way to group frequently used items.

HARDWARE, MANUAL, AND CHARGER STORAGE

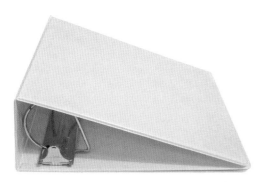

1 LARGE BINDERS

Binders are for more than just office reports. If you get creative and think about what other ways you can use them around your home, you might come up with some really unique organization and storage opportunities. Here, a binder is home to a quick and easy way to organize your electronic devices.

2 STORAGE BAGS

Choose high-quality plastic food storage bags with a zipper-lock seal when storing heavier items like manuals, chargers, and other miscellaneous cords and accessories. Use a couple different sizes to hold a variety of items.

3 MANILA FOLDERS

Repurpose these everyday folders to provide structure in your hardware binder.

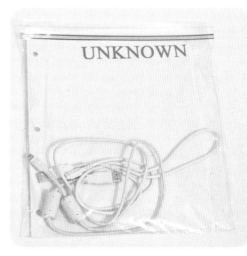

4 LABELS

Easy-to-read lables placed in a prominent spot let you see at a glance what you have.

Handy Hardware Binder

The more electronic equipment you have, the more cords, chargers, cables, and other accessories you have to go along with them. Cell phones, computers, tablets, MP3 players—each comes with its own specific cables and cords, and organizing all those items can be a challenge. Not anymore. This quick and easy project helps you organize all those items once and for all.

DIY PROJECT #15

MATERIALS

4-INCH (10CM) THREE-RING BINDER

1-QUART (1L) PLASTIC RESEALABLE BAGS

1-GALLON (3.75L) PLASTIC RESEALABLE BAGS

MANILA FOLDER

LABEL PAPER

TOOLS

SCISSORS

PRINTER

THREE-HOLE PUNCH

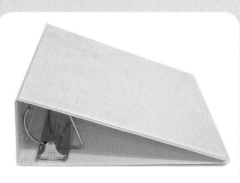

I used a 4-inch (10cm) three-ring binder to organize my family's electronic device hardware and 12 1-quart (1l) plastic resealable bags and two 1-gallon (3.75l) plastic resealable bags to hold the accessories. I cut a manila folder to fit inside each size of bag for strength, printed labels for each device, and placed the label on the folder. I tucked the folders inside the bags and punched holes through both the bag and the folder using a three-hole punch.

For easiest access, I punched the holes at the bottom of the plastic bags so the opening is at the edge of the binder.

As I added the bags to the binder, I alternated the placement, attaching one bag on the top two rings and the next on the bottom two rings to distribute the bulk and also show the labels. To each bag, I added instructions, USB cables, chargers, and any other accessories for each device, putting the most frequently used bags at the front of the binder.

In the back, I added another 1-gallon (3.75l) plastic resealable bag for unknown cables, chargers, and accessories.

Now all our cables and cords are in one easy-to-find location! For more information, visit thecreativityexchange.com/organizing-your-life.

after

TRICK #1
RETHINK THUMBTACKS

In addition to holding paper and small office supplies on your bulletin board, you can use larger thumbtacks or nail heads to attach small wall storage containers to your bulletin board. The larger head of the tack or nail provides a sturdy foundation for your container.

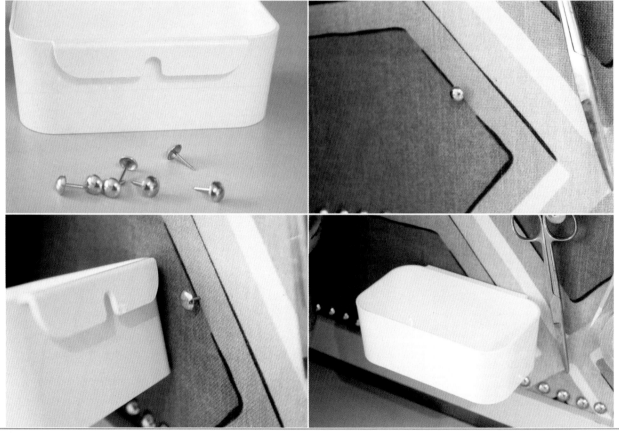

QUICK TRICKS

TRICK #2
WALL POCKETS

Adhere wall pockets or other deep and narrow storage containers above and beside your desk to hold items up and off your desktop. These organizers are inexpensive and easy to hang using nails or screws.

CHECKLIST

notes

storage pieces

quick tricks

inspiration

CENTSATIONALGIRL.COM

THECREATIVITYEXCHANGE.COM

tips

- On the wall either in front of your desk (if your desk is against the wall) or near your desk, install wall command centers with bulletin boards, wall pockets for papers, and shelving.

- Employ office storage carts with drawers on wheels to instantly add storage and improve efficiency. You can roll the cart back into a closet or corner after you're done with it.

- Maximize your office wall space by using floor-to-ceiling shelving or bookshelves instead of storage pieces that only go halfway up the wall. This can *double* your amount of storage!

- Consider dedicating a drawer in your desk as your inbox to keep the top of your desk free from papers at all times.

- House a large bin on wheels next to your desk for tossing items that can be sorted later to keep your work area free from clutter.

- Install cube or cubby storage pieces along the wall or in a cabinet (you might have to remove a shelf) for easy compartmental storage for little stuff.

- Assess your trouble spots. Look around your desk and office area and determine what items do not have a home. It helps to think of these items as they relate to a specific office task and then create organized storage solutions grouped around specific tasks—printer, printer supplies, paper supplies, etc. all organized together, for example.

- Use rectangular planter boxes in a cabinet or on a shelf to stack notebooks, folders, and files you can quickly access.

- Set an old dresser or hutch next to a desk for additional storage for office supplies, books, and files. For a quick update, add a fresh coat of paint.

MULTI-PURPOSE ROOM

Count yourself lucky if you have a room in your home you and your family are able to use for multiple purposes. However, you might not feel so lucky about all the supplies, equipment, tools, and other items that relate to the tasks and activities done within this room—especially when they're an unorganized mess.

In this section, I share a multipurpose room that serves as a family room, a playroom, a craft room, and an office—all in one space. By designating each corner of the room for a specific task and creating multipurpose storage solutions, you can keep your multipurpose room from feeling messy and cluttered.

1 **TABLE AND STORAGE OTTOMANS**
A table in the center of a multipurpose room can be the center of the activity. Place a tray on the tabletop in which to toss items, or add a decorative vase if you want to keep this area clutter free. Use ottomans to replace the chairs and provide seating as well as storage.

2 **STORAGE OTTOMAN COFFEE TABLE**
If your multipurpose room has space for a lounge area, add a large storage ottoman to hold blankets and pillows and do double-duty as a coffee table.

3 **HIDDEN STORAGE**
Add doors to open cabinets to give your room hidden storage options. This is especially key in multipurpose spaces because of the different tasks and activities the area is used for. Designate bins and baskets for specific supplies and tuck them in the cabinet for quick cleanup.

4 **COUNTERSPACE OPTIONS**
If your room is large enough to hold a countertop, employ small jars, bowls, and baskets to combat clutter there. Consider, too, adding shelves above the counter to make the most of your space.

1 **GLASS JARS**
Group together a few clear glass jars, and fill them with small brushes, spools of thread, craft supplies, or other small items you need to be able to locate quickly.

2 **VASES**
If you have surplus floral vases, use them for organizing pens, paintbrushes, and similar skinny things on the counter or shelves for easy access.

3 **BASKETS**
Decorative baskets are must-haves on shelves and countertops. Choose pretty yet practical baskets with handles so you can load them up and easily take them wherever you need to go.

4 **CLEAR PLASTIC ORGANIZERS**
Clear plastic organizers can hold myriad items in one place. These inexpensive storage solutions enable you to group items like together in different-size compartments.

Inexpensive Built-Ins

If you've always wanted the look and functionally of custom-designed built-ins but thought they were out of your budget, this project is for you. By using inexpensive premade stock kitchen cabinets and planning your space around standard-width sizes of MDF board/wood (so no special cuts are needed), you'll be pleasantly surprised how affordable built-ins can be!

MATERIALS

PREMADE STOCK CABINETS

SHEETS OF MDF BOARD/PLYWOOD

WOOD SHELVING BOARDS

SCREWS

NAILS

PAINT

TOOLS

PENCIL

TAPE MEASURE

STUD FINDER

SAW

HAMMER

DRILL

DRILL BITS

PAINTBRUSH

PAINTER'S TAPE

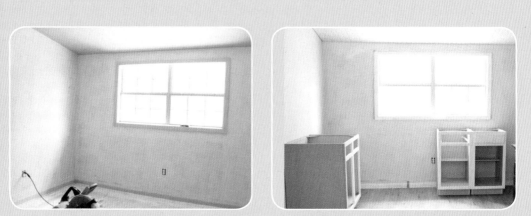

I opted for unfinished stock kitchen cabinets from my local big-box home improvement store as the base of my built-ins. I used one large double-door base cabinet, two single-door bases, and one double-door upper cabinet. A quick coat of paint is all they needed to look more custom-designed.

DO IT YOURSELF

Building the shelving, which eventually would go up on the wall, on the floor first made construction easier.

Then I moved the shelves up onto the counter (which was plywood cut to fit—one of the few special cuts necessary) and attached the whole frame to the wall.

I used the wall as the backing of the cabinets instead of adding more wood there to save even more money. More paint helped create a consistent, unified look.

Designing and installing custom built-ins and shelving doesn't have to be a large investment, thanks to some careful planning and smart design. For more how-to information and inspirational photos, visit thecreativityexchange.com/organizing-your-life.

after

CREATIVE
DRAWER STORAGE

You can create organizing opportunities in drawers in your family's multipurpose room to fit what your family likes to do, the activities you spend time on, or the items you'll find most helpful to corral in a drawer in this space. Here are some examples of drawers you can consider.

1 GIFT-GIVING DRAWER

Create a drawer for gift-wrap-related items to hold gift tags, labels, favor bags, and cards in one spot. This helps you keep all the little gift-related things organized and within easy reach when you need to give a gift.

2 HARDWARE DRAWER

Dedicate a drawer to corralling hardware and small tools to organize nails, screws, wall-hanging hardware, hooks, tape measures, and other small items. Use inexpensive plastic bead organizers with the lids removed, desk drawer organizers, or even ice cube trays—anything that offers small compartments you need.

3 KID'S CRAFT SUPPLIES DRAWER

Set aside one drawer specifically for your child's craft supplies. This gives your little one his or her own space for their stuff, provides a chance for you to share the same area but not necessarily the same supplies, and allows you an opportunity to teach your youngsters about organizing.

4 SEWING SUPPLIES DRAWER

Make a drawer for all the little sewing notions and supplies you need to sew on a button, repair a hole, or tack up a hem so you can find these items quickly. Combine your sewing supplies with daily household essentials like rubber bands, safety pins, scissors, and straight pins, and you make this drawer a dual-purpose one.

CREATIVE
CABINET STORAGE

1 CRAFT SUPPLY STORAGE

Customizing a cabinet for hobby supplies—whatever your hobbies might be—not only groups these supplies in one area but also can become your workstation so you never have to carry your tools or supplies elsewhere to work. Use stackable bins to hold different pieces and parts, and hang hooks, baskets, and other storage pieces on the inside of the cabinet doors for easy access.

2 **KID'S ACTIVITY STORAGE**

Whatever activities your child loves to do, you can give them a space in the multipurpose room and create something special just for them. Add cube storage, shelves, baskets, and bins to hold their supplies, and when they open the doors at playtime, everything they need for fun is right at their fingertips. When play-time is over, you can simply close the cabinet doors.

Closed Door Storage

Built-in bookshelves are wonderful if you have the space and budget to create them. But if you have too many open shelving systems in a room, the area can start to feel cluttered, even if they're all neatly organized. By adding cabinet doors to an existing open cabinet (as I'll show you here), built-in shelving, or even a bookshelf, you can close the door on clutter.

MATERIALS

SQUARE-EDGE TRIM   HINGES

FINISHING NAILS   SCREWS

SPACKLE   PAINT

PRIMER

SHEETS OF MDF
BOARD

TOOLS

CROWBAR   TAPE MEASURE

HAMMER   SAW

PUTTY KNIFE   SCREWDRIVER

PAINTBRUSH

I started by removing the inside shelves and all the contents of my cabinet.

My cabinet had trim with a rounded edge around the frame. That wouldn't be flush with the front and sides of the doors I wanted to add, so I removed it with a small crowbar.

I added new trim with square edges using finishing nails. I patched the nail holes with spackle, and when the spackle was dry, I added a coat of primer.

I measured my cabinet opening to find the size I needed for my cabinet doors and cut them out of MDF board to ensure the side edges were smooth and the doors wouldn't warp over time. When measuring the cabinet frame to get the size I needed for my cabinet doors, I planned that the hinges and trim edge would be flush when the doors were opened.

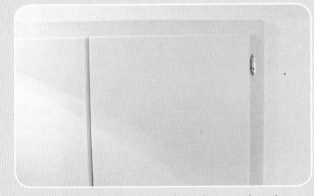

I installed the hinges, attached the doors to the cabinet, and gave everything a coat of paint.

after

Now this area of my multipurpose room still has the feel of a custom-built piece, but the cabinet doors give me the option of closing away what's behind them. For more how-to information and inspirational photos, visit thecreativityexchange.com/organizing-your-life.

GIFT WRAPPING STATION

1 CABINETS

Installing inexpensive premade stock cabinets is a quick and easy way to create more storage space. Inside, I turned mail organizers on their side to create slotted compartments for note cards, envelopes, and other paper storage.

2 MAGAZINE HOLDERS

Tucked into my cabinet, magazine holders keep gift bags and wrapping paper neat and orderly. By storing the bags upright, I can see what I have at a glance, and I can store many items together in a compact area.

3 WIRE BASKETS

Wire baskets enable you to organize items neatly yet still the basket contents. By using containers you can see through, you cut down on the time you'd spend trying to find certain items later. If you don't like having these transparent containers out in the open, tuck them behind closed doors.

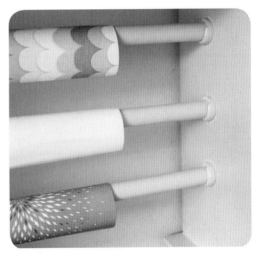

4 CLOSET RODS

If you keep rolls of wrapping paper on hand, you might find that standing them up in a corner can lead to wrinkled or torn paper. Instead, organize the rolls on closet rods. Use adjustable rods, or cut them to fit your space. Hang them with the open part of the brackets all facing up so you can pop out the rod easily when you need to.

TRICK #1

REPURPOSE INEXPENSIVE BEAD ORGANIZERS

Try this quick trick when you need to drawer storage: instead of purchasing pricier hardware storage organizers, opt for inexpensive plastic bead organizers instead. You may leave the lid on if you have several to stack in a space. Or cut off the lid for easily accessible open storage compartments. Use a small pair of sharp scissors to cut the plastic hinges. When the lid has been removed, you can cut the plastic even closer to the storage tray if you need to. Now you have the perfect storage solution for all your nails, screws, tacks, and other little hardware pieces.

TRICK #2
RETHINK SCRAPBOOK PAPER

If you've been to a craft store lately, you might know how very many colors and patterns scrapbook paper comes in. For a quick and easy drawer liner, pick up a few pieces of thick cardstock scrapbook paper, cut it to fit your drawers, and install using glue dots or double-sided tape. If you want, you can laminate the paper before installing it for extra durability and easier cleanup.

CHECKLIST

MULTIPURPOSE ROOM

notes

storage pieces

quick tricks

inspiration

THECREATIVITYEXCHANGE.COM

tips

- Opt for floor-to-ceiling storage pieces that fill the whole wall to create the most storage.

- In the middle of the room, house tables, storage ottomans, or multitiered roller carts for ongoing projects.

- Choose baskets and bins that make the most of the height available inside cabinets or open shelving to increase your amount of storage.

- Use glass containers and canisters to organize the little stuff so you can instantly spot what you need.

- Select the same color and style of baskets to help contain the little stuff and make the room look cohesive with all the different tasks performed there.

- Implement drawer storage under where the specific task will be done to organize all the supplies required for that task while keeping the open areas free of clutter.

- Assess your trouble spots. To determine what needs to be contained in a multipurpose space, make a list of four or five of your family's greatest spatial needs that you currently lack. Draw your room on paper with to-scale measurements, and look for creative ways to incorporate these tasks into each corner and in the middle of the room. Start with the measurements of the furniture you have, or will have in the room, first. Everything else will fall into place around those pieces, and you can calculate the measurements you need for storage and additional pieces.

- Incorporate furniture taking up space elsewhere your home in your multipurpose room if it has organizing potential. An old desk can become an office, a hutch can be transformed into a media center, or a table can be set in the center of the room for activities and eating. Paint these pieces the same color as your other storage pieces for a cohesive look.

GARAGE

It's all too easy to let the garage become a catch-all for whatever you don't want in your house, haphazardly tossing excess stuff into that out-of-the way space with no thought given to organization. Or you might have the opposite problem—maybe your garage is completely empty and untapped for potential storage possibilities because you're at a loss for how to come up with creative garage storage solutions.

Whether you're looking to get organized and unclutter your garage or you have a bare garage begging for organization, in this section, you learn tips to address both extremes and discover how to create and inexpensive long-term organizing solutions that can inspire you to get your garage organized once and for all.

THE
GARAGE

1 **PEGBOARD TOOL STORAGE**
Pegboard is an easy, inexpensive, and long-term solution for storing tools and other garage equipment. Because of its compact design, pegboard can be a realistic solution even in very narrow spaces.

2 **PEGBOARD TOY STORAGE**
Pegboard isn't just for tools. Getting toys and sports equipment off the garage floor and onto a pegboard storage wall is a great way to control garage clutter. Hang them on hooks placed low enough for kids to reach, and you create an easy-access activity station.

3 **CLOSED STORAGE**

Not all garage storage has to be out in the open. Storage cabinets and shelving are ideal for containing items in the garage. These tall units fill the wall space from the floor to the ceiling and are sold in shallow depths to fit in narrow areas.

4 **MOBILE TOOL STORAGE**

In addition to corralling tools in the garage, chest-style toolboxes can be used for craft or hobby supply storage or just about anything else you need to store. And because they're set on wheels, you can move them around to your work area.

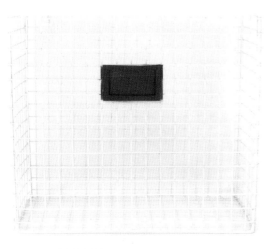

1 MAGNETIC BOARD

Cover a thin sheet of metal with vinyl or durable fabric for a quick and easy magnetic board you can use to hold lots of little stuff.

Galvanized pails hung on hooks are another option.

2 STORAGE CABINETS

Small drawer storage cabinets designed to hold nails, screws, nuts, and bolts don't have to take up valuable space on your workbench. Hang the cabinet on a pegboard wall instead.

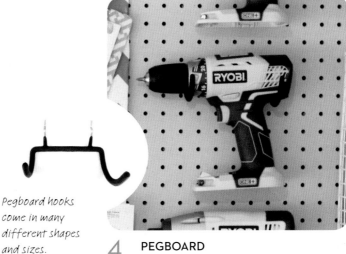

3 WIRE BINS

Hang wire bins of various sizes and shapes anywhere and everywhere you need to corral miscellaneous items in your garage.

Pegboard hooks come in many different shapes and sizes.

4 PEGBOARD

A quick coat of paint turns a sheet of pegboard installed on a garage wall into a clean and cohesive storage wall.

Pegboard Storage Wall

The garage often is home to lots of tools, gadgets, supplies, and equipment. With so much "stuff," organization and storage can be a challenge. As this project shows, you don't need a lot of space to create a smart solution for just about any area. This pegboard storage unit is only $5^1/_2$ inches (14cm) deep. I designed and built it using 1×6-inch (2.5×15cm) pine boards.

MATERIALS

1×6-INCH (2.5×15CM) BOARDS

1×2-INCH (2.5×5CM) BOARDS

4×8-FOOT (1.25×2.5M) PEG-BOARD SHEETS

SCREWS

NAILS

CAULK

PAINT

PEGS AND HOOKS

BASKETS, BUCKETS, AND OTHER STORAGE PIECES

TOOLS

PENCIL

TAPE MEASURE

STUD FINDER

HAMMER

SAW

DRILL

DRILL BITS

CAULKING GUN

PAINTBRUSH

PAINTER'S TAPE

1×2-inch (2.5×5cm) support

I only had a narrow space in the garage to work with and still have enough room for two cars to fit as well, but the wall is rather large: 12 feet (3.5m) wide from the door on the left to the corner on the right and 8 feet (2.5m) tall.

I attached a 1×2-inch (2.5×5cm) board where I wanted the bottom shelf to be. This served as a support for the shelf and gave me something to which to secure the shelf. I then nailed the 1×6-inch (2.5×15cm) shelf board to the support. I attached the sides, two more 1×6-inch (2.5×15cm) boards, nailing them to the 1×2-inch (2.5×5cm) support and also to the shelf.

The 1×2-inch (2.5×5cm) boards behind the pegboard hold it out from the wall so you can insert pegs and hooks into the pegboard. Don't nail the pegboard to the wall, or you won't be able to insert the pegs correctly.

I added more 1×2-inch (2.5×5cm) boards to support more shelves and to have a surface to which to nail the pegboard: inside the frame next to the sides, where I planned to put two more 1×6-inch (2.5×15cm) shelves above and below the pegboards, down the center, and where the two panels met. Using two 4×8-foot (1.25×2.5m) pegboard panels, cutting one to fit, I nail them to the supports.

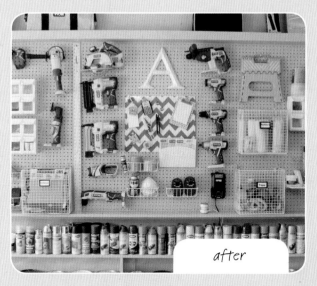

after

I caulked the edges of the unit and painted the wall and the rest of the wood. (Caulking along the edges where the wood meets the wall makes the piece look more like a professionally crafted built-in unit.) To help keep the items on the top shelf in place, I added a final 1×2-inch (2.5×5cm) board to the edge of the top shelf to serve as a lip.

You can use a pegboard for storing almost everything, and with so many unique pegboard hooks available, you can hang just about anything. This project isn't limited to the garage. It could be used in a basement, closet, or anywhere else you have a spare wall and lots of smaller items to organize. For more how-to information and photos, visit thecreativityexchange.com/organizing-your-life.

1 HANGING BASKETS

Pegboard baskets, bins, hooks and other accessories are so varied and plentiful, you're sure to be ablet to find just the organizational pieces you need for your family.

Buckets hanging on a hook are a great alternative to bins and containers.

2 CHALKBOARD LABELS

Labels are an organizer's best friend. By spray painter's tape with black chalkboard paint, you can create easy chalkboard labels. Let the tape dry, cut to fit your container, and write on it with chalk.

3 BASKETS

Baskets come in all shapes and sizes. Placing certain items in baskets with handles makes carrying those items easier.

4 BINS ON WHEELS

Store outside toys and sports equipment in large bins on wheels to make them easy to roll out to the play area and then back to the garage afterward.

TRICK #1

MAKE A QUICK AND EASY MAGNETIC BOARD

Assemble an instant-fabric covered magnetic board by cutting a square or rectangular piece of metal sheeting (available at home improvement stores) and covering it with fabric. Cut your fabric a a bit larger than your sheet of metal (about 2 inches; 5cm) so you can wrap it around the edges and secure it on the back side. Place your fabric right side down on your work surface, and add the metal piece on top. Starting in the middle of one side, begin to evenly fold the fabric over the edge of the metal to the back side and use a hot glue gun to adhere the fabric to the back, being sure to pull the fabric taught and smooth. Nail the board to the pegboard wall in the garage, or insert the metal into a frame and hang inside your house. Use large magnets to attach clipboards, clips, pens, and other smaller items to the magnetic board.

TRICK #2
CREATE CHALKBOARD LABELS

Making chalkboard labels to use in the garage (or anywhere!) is simple thanks to a can of spray paint and painter's tape. Attach a long strip of painter's tape to something you don't mind getting paint on such as an old birdcage frame, spray the nonsticky side of the strip of tape with black flat spray paint or chalkboard paint, and let it dry completely. When the tape is dry, you can cut your labels and attach then wherever you like. The painter's tape, as opposed to packing tape, makes the label easier to remove later if you like. To write on the labels, use chalk or a chalk pen. (If you use chalk, slightly wet it first and the letters will be bolder.)

CHECKLIST   GARAGE

notes

storage pieces

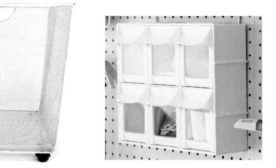

quick tricks

inspiration

THECREATIVITYEXCHANGE.COM

tips

- Install pegboard or narrow shelving solutions on bare walls to hang tools, yard supplies, or auto equipment.

- Measure your cars when they're parked in the garage to better see where you have wasted space and potential storage possibilities.

- Look at ways to maximize the garage walls from the floor all the way to the ceiling. Purchase narrow metal shelving, or construct your own narrow plywood shelving.

- Set stackable plastic or metal bins in a corner or by the door into the house for tossing little stuff.

- Attach hooks to the walls to hang metal buckets or baskets with handles for storing pet leashes and supplies, tool and craft supplies, or almost anything.

- Arrange cube or cubby storage pieces along the wall to provide compartmental storage for sporting equipment, pet supplies, or other smaller items.

- Assess your trouble spots. As you organize your garage, take a close look at what items need a dedicated storage spot. Similar to other areas in your home, group like items together when creating storage solutions—gardening supplies together, tools together, household supplies together, etc. When you have these items divided into categories, you can see how much storage space you'll need for the group, and you can begin to come up with long-term storage solutions for these items.

- Hang an old bulletin board or large frame converted into a bulletin board in the garage right next to the door going into the house for notes, messages, or lists.

- Repurpose an old narrow bookshelf or shelving unit taking up space elsewhere in your home in the garage for storing bins or garage supplies.

THE REST OF YOUR LIFE

The same key elements and processes that go into successfully organizing your home apply to organizing the rest of your life, too. Instead of maximizing your space, however, think of organizing your life as maximizing your time. Instead of looking for areas of wasted physical space, look for wasted spots in your life needlessly taking up your time and energy. And as you purge items you no longer need or want from your home, purge those things in your life that are no longer important or serve a purpose.

The challenging part of this is that organizing the rest of your life isn't as easy—nor as fast—as organizing your kitchen pantry, for example. However, if you change your focus and the way you think about organizing and throw away any preconceived notions and unrealistic visions of organizing perfection, you can start fresh and begin to look for realistic ways to get and stay organized in all areas of your life.

◀ photo credit: evolutionofstyleblog.blogspot.com

AN ORGANIZED LIFE

Organizing your life is not impossible. In fact, it's very doable, and it's probably a lot closer than you think.

ONE THING AT A TIME

When you're organizing your home, you know you need to resist the urge to compile a long and intimidating list of all the areas in that need to be organized. The same is true when you set about to organize your life.

Instead, focus on solving one problem at a time so you don't get overwhelmed by all the issues and tasks you need to get in order. Just the thought of everything you need to get sorted and straightened can be enough to make you want to give up before you start. If you keep it simple, you stand a greater chance of succeeding because you reduce the intimidation such a large task can cause.

When you work on one problem at a time, you inadvertently create a chain reaction in other areas of your life. If you find ways to better manage your time or purge things from your life that waste the most time, you create more time for other areas in your life.

IDENTIFY PROBLEM AREAS

An important element for successful organizing, whether it be in your home or your life, is stepping back and assessing your trouble spots. Without pinpointing the exact source of the problem, it's hard to know what type of a solution you need to fix it for the long term.

For example, instead of looking in general at ways to better manage your time, pinpoint the source of where you waste the most amount of time—the laundry room, the office, etc. Then take an honest look at what specific tasks in those areas are draining your time so you can begin to find a solution.

PURGING VERSUS TIME MANAGEMENT

When it comes to organizing your life, it's only natural to assume better time management is the first place to start. Managing your time efficiently is important, but the real solution is often found by purging things from your life that waste your time and, therefore, weigh you down.

So many of us try to fit twice as much stuff into our days than we actually have time for. It's just like trying to organize an overstuffed closet that contains twice as many clothes as available closet space. We won't see results in the closet if we don't get rid of clothes we no longer need. The same is true in your life. What can you take off your to-do list?

LIVING THE LIFE YOU LOVE

Purging things from your life isn't an easy task, especially when you have a busy family and feel pressure to take on more than you have time to do. Oftentimes, we take on things out of obligation or because it's hard to say no, which compounds that feeling of being out of control of our life. Something has to give!

Implementing a strategy for determining what you should take on and when you need to say no makes all the difference—and it makes purging so much easier.

If you take on tasks you enjoy and eliminate those things that drain you and no longer serve a purpose in your life, you'll find you have more enthusiasm, energy, and time. And most importantly, you'll be happier. Asking yourself *Do I love it?* when looking at what to purge, or *Will I love it?* when asked to take on something is the best way to assess what needs to stay and what needs to go. If the answer to either question is no, you can walk away.

You purge your closets and home based on what pieces you love and don't love, but for some reason, it's not always obvious that you need to make that same connection when it comes to organizing your life. Your time is precious, and your happiness is the primary goal. Focusing on what makes you happy should be the basis for how you go about getting your life organized.

PULLING IT ALL TOGETHER

As you begin to look at ways to organize your life, remember to tackle one problem at a time by assessing your trouble spots and clearly identifying the source of the problem areas—it's impossible to come up with solutions if you don't first identify what's wrong. Instead of looking for ways to make more time for the stuff that ultimately weighs you down, focus your energy on assessing the value of what you're doing and how you're spending your time. Too often, what you feel or think is organizational problem in your life is actually more about taking on too much and spending too much of your limited time doing things you don't love.

Organizing your life and living the life you love won't happen overnight, but if you begin asking yourself *Do I love it?* or *Will I love it?* you'll begin to see and feel that you are, in fact, in control. There's a great relief that comes with knowing you finally have a realistic strategy and plan for getting organized.

TO-DO LISTS

With busy families and busy lives, keeping track of everything you need to do day in and day out can get overwhelming, and staying a step ahead of the chaos can be a challenge.

What's more, if you're not a "list person," you might have the best intentions and start a to-do list … but then forget to update it, lose it, start a separate list, or let it get so out of control it's no longer an aid in helping you get organized but rather something *else* you have to get in order.

It doesn't have to be that way. By creating a customized to-do list that covers just about everything in your day or week, you can look ahead, think about what you need to do before the chaos hits, and better keep track of everything you need to keep track of. As a bonus, this advance planning helps you spot any problems or issues ahead of time.

MAKING MY LIST

Several years ago, I designed my own to-do list that included a section for all the tasks I anticipated I needed to get through during my day. I thought that if I was going to make myself use a list, it wouldn't just be a partial list but rather a full and complete list that included *everything* I needed to do, buy, pick up, drop off, etc. The more value I could add to the list, the more I would rely on it—and actually *use* it.

I also told myself that I would do the list ahead of time either for the week or the day, depending how busy I was. At the end of the day, when I finally got caught up or had a moment to spare, I would update the list.

This way, I planned my day ahead of time, but I still had the list to be my guide and keep me on track and organized. This method has worked well for me.

MAKING YOUR LIST

The best way to make the most of a to-do list is to design your own list customized to the tasks you do during your days and weeks.

You can create your list on your computer using a blank word processing document, or you can keep it in a notebook or on your smartphone. It doesn't have to be a fancy or pretty list, just something that helps you plot out your week or day.

For inspiration when designing your own to-do list, feel free to look at mine. It's available for free download at thecreativityexchange.com/organizing-your-life. Download the file and either customize my template by typing in your own section titles, or use the titles on my list if they work for you. You can always try my list and customize it later as you discover what works best for you and your family.

If you keep your list out in the open for the whole family to see, they might be able to help you complete some of the tasks. In addition, everyone will be able to see what your day looks like and how busy you'll be.

Printable To-Do Lists

A to-do list can help keep you incredibly organized. But it's far too easy to have one list on a sticky note in your wallet, another on your smartphone, another on your computer, etc. Having all your to-do items in one spot is so much better—and ensures you're more likely to actually remember everything on your list.

MATERIALS

8½×11-INCH (21.5×28CM) LABEL PAPER

TOOLS

PRINTER

This easy-to-use list is available online for you to download and start using it immediately. To use the list, go to thecreativityexchange.com/organizing-your-life, and download the blank to-do list template. Either print the list on 8½×11-inch (21.5×28cm) paper and write on it with a pen or pencil, or fill in the list on your computer using image-editing software and then print.

This to-do list really helps me keep my days on track. I hope it does the same for you! For more information, visit thecreativityexchange.com/organizing-your-life.

To Do Today

Need to Go Here and Pick Up

_____ _____
_____ _____
_____ _____
_____ _____
_____ _____
                         _____

Groceries

Clean This

_____ _____
_____ _____
_____ _____
_____ _____
_____ _____
_____ _____
_____ _____
_____ _____
_____ _____
_____ _____

Be There

_____ @ ___:___
_____ @ ___:___
_____ @ ___:___

Cook This

_____
_____
_____

Email:

Call:

Text:

PURGE AND DECLUTTER

Although necessary, purging and decluttering can be a difficult task. It's far too easy to become attached to your stuff and not want to part with it—that's likely what lead to the clutter and lack of organization in the first place. Deciding what to keep and what to part with—especially those items you have an emotional or sentimental attachment to—can become overwhelming quickly.

The key to efficiently sorting and eliminating items you no longer need is establishing a system for determining what stays and what goes— quickly and without the agony of indecision. If you set up a sort-and-purge routine monthly or seasonally, you'll really see a decrease in the amount of "stuff" in your home and in your life.

In this section, I share my method of purging and decluttering.

FIRST SWEEP

For the first sweep, you'll need three large plastic storage bins, cardboard boxes, or trash bags. Designate two of them for what you normally do with your purged items—if you donate your items, designate one bin for donation; if you give away your items to a sister or family member, designate the bin for that. Designate the third bin for "uncertain" items.

Now do a first sweep of your cabinet, closet, or room. During this first pass, remove those items you have no attachment to, those items you don't hesitate to put in the "get rid of" bin.

If you have to think about something for more than 10 seconds, set it aside in the "uncertain" bin for now and move on to the next item. You'll revisit those uncertain items on the second sweep.

Resist the urge to first organize the space you're about to declutter. This is unnecessary, wastes time, and provides too many opportunities for you to get sidetracked. Stay focused on sorting and eliminating.

SECOND SWEEP

After you've gone through your first sweep, do a second sweep. This time, focus on those "uncertain" items you hesitated on the first time. Often, these pieces are clothing, accessories, or other things you haven't worn or used for years, yet they remain in your closet, taking up space. Or maybe they're items of clothing (if you're purging a closet) that no longer fit or have sentimental value.

If you're purging a closet, don't stop to try on clothes now to determine if a piece needs to stay or go. This is just another opportunity for you to get sidetracked. Save trying on clothes for a different day. For now, toss any questionable items into the uncertain bin or a separate "try on" bin.

DEAL WITH THE STORAGE BINS

As soon as you've gone through the space two times, place the bins that contain items to get rid of or donate to someone else in your car for immediate drop-off. Or if you don't have a car, place them by your front door or somewhere where you can deal with them quickly and not be tempted to let them linger.

Relocate the uncertain bin somewhere like an attic or basement—someplace far enough away so you won't be tempted to revisit the items and put them back where they were before. If you can go a month or two without needing those items, you'll be better able to admit to yourself that you can get rid of them permanently. If you do discover you really need an item in the bin, you still have it and can get it out of the bin.

After you have purged your home or closet the first time using this method, begin your next sort-and-purge session by going through the uncertain bin and make room for the new items you might want to place there.

MAKE IT A REGULAR ROUTINE

This method of purging and decluttering helps you get into a regular routine. Over time, you'll see how this process can have a major impact on helping you get—and stay—organized.

PRINTABLES

Throughout the book I've shared some of my favorite printables I've designed—labels, worksheets, to-do lists, etc. These have helped me tremendously as I have organized my kitchen, bathrooms, closets, and so much more, and I hope they do the same for you.

I've assembled them all here so you can find them quickly and easily. All you need to create these printables is some $8\frac{1}{2}\times11$-inch (21.5×28cm) copy paper or $8\frac{1}{2}\times11$-inch (21.5×28cm) label paper, a printer, scissors, and maybe a pen or marker if you choose the blank labels. Download the files from my website at thecreativityexchange.com/organizing-your-life, and you'll be able to print your own pretty labels and lists for use anywhere and everywhere!

PRINTABLES

PRINTABLE BOOKMARK

You might be surprised how often you pick up this bookmark. Use it to mark pages you want to come back to, pages that hold pictures of items you want to purchase, or the DIY sections you want to try.

#1

HELPFUL HINTS

· focus on one problem at a time
· assess your trouble spots
· look for areas of wasted space
· choose storage that maximizes space
· find creative solutions

NOTES:

PRINTABLE BAKING/PANTRY CABINET LABELS

These pretty, fun labels are perfect for organizing your baking cabinet, pantry, or any other spot where you have multiple containers that need a little dressing up.

PRINTABLE BATHROOM LABELS

These multipurpose labels can go on items in your medicine cabinet—or just about anywhere else you can think to use them!

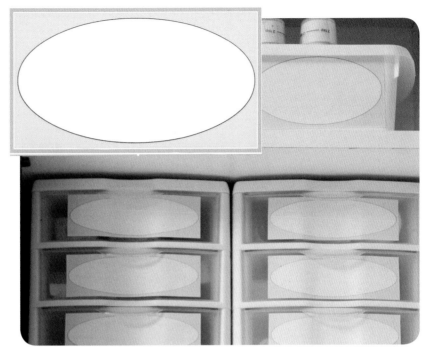

PRINTABLE NURSERY LABELS

I showed you these fun labels in the nursery section, adhered to small buckets, but you can use them anywhere you need a pop of color.

PRINTABLE CLOSET
ORGANIZATION WORKSHEET

Organizing closets can be hard enough. Make the task easier by first planning out what you want to do in your closet by using this handy worksheet.

Closet Organization Worksheet

Organizing a closet can be a daunting task, especially if you have more stuff than available closet space. Having a plan before you begin working, however, can make all the difference.

1 USING A PENCIL (NOT A PEN), DRAW A ROUGH SKETCH OF THE INSIDE OF YOUR CLOSET:

2 RANK, IN ORDER, YOUR CLOSET'S TOP THREE PROBLEMS:

____ not enough space for shoes

____ not enough space for handbags

____ not enough space for accessories

____ not enough drawer space

____ not enough hanging space

____ not enough space to hang pants

____ not enough space to hang long pieces

____ too many clothes

____ other _____

3 LOOK AT YOUR TOP THREE TROUBLE SPOTS, DETERMINE WHAT YOU NEED TO SOLVE THOSE PROBLEMS, AND RANK THEM IN ORDER:

____ more hanging space

____ more drawer space

____ more storage space for shoes

____ more storage space for handbags

____ more storage space for folded items

____ more storage space for accessories

____ more space for clothes hamper

____ more hanging space for _____

____ more shelving for _____

____ more specialized storage for _____

____ other _____

4 Determine what areas of your closet are wasted space or spots where you could create new organization opportunities. Circle these areas on your sketch. Then ask yourself:

- What areas am I currently not maximizing?
- Could I move any storage pieces currently in my closet to other areas if they work better somewhere else?
- What hanging pieces could I move around or add to maximize the space available?

5 Go back to your closet and measure the areas you circled on your sketch. Write these dimensions on your sketch.

6 Determine what color storage pieces will best coordinate with the trim and shelving in your closet. Note that if you choose any color other than white, dark brown, or black, you might have some difficulty finding standard storage pieces.

7 Search online for new storage pieces. Be sure to carefully check dimensions and look for color options that are close to your trim/shelving color. Also try to make the most of your space available by choosing storage pieces that are functional and won't leave you with any wasted space. Bookmark or list here the storage pieces you're interested in:

_____
_____
_____
_____
_____
_____

8 Draw the potential new storage pieces in your sketch of your closet, and erase and move any existing storage changes you can make. This helps you come to a decision on what storage pieces you should purchase.

9 Purge your closet of any unwanted items. A good rule of thumb is if you haven't worn it or used it for a year, get rid of it.

10 Instead of empting out your whole closet to begin your reorganization, work section by section, incorporating and filling new storage pieces as you go. This way you can step away from reorganizing for a day or two and not be tempted to just give up and put everything back where it was.

11 As you finish adding your new storage pieces, take note of areas where you could employ more baskets, bins, and other special smaller pieces to keep your closet organized—for good.

PRINTABLE
TO-DO LISTS

Be honest. How many to-do lists do you have right now—in your purse, in your pocket, on sticky notes stuck everywhere, on your smartphone? Keep all your to-dos organized on this helpful list.

To Do Today		

Need to Go Here	and	Pick Up

Groceries		Clean This

Be There		Cook This

@ ___ : ___

@ ___ : ___

@ ___ : ___

Email:	Call:	Text:

PHOTO CREDITS

Photography by Cyndy Aldred, with the following exceptions: